Rudy's Rules

RUDY'S RULES

by Rudy Ruettiger
and Mike Celizic

WRS
PUBLISHING

A Division of WRS Group, Inc.
Waco, Texas

First published in the United States of America in 1995 by WRS Publishing,
A Division of WRS Group, Inc., 701 N. New Road, Waco, Texas 76710
Book design by Yvonne Chiu and Kenneth Turbeville
Jacket design by Joe James

10 9 8 7 6 5 4 3 2 1

Library of Congress Cataloging-in-Publication Data

Ruettiger, Rudy
    Rudy's Rules / by Rudy Ruettiger and Mike Celizic
        p.   cm.
    ISBN 1-56796-056-1 : $19.95
    1. Success.   2. Conduct of life   I. Celizic, Mike.   II. Title.
BJ1611.2.R84   1994
158'.1--dc20   94-21231
                                                        CIP

Dedication

To Mom, Dad, Jean Ann, Mary, Carol, Rose, Betsy, Timmy, Francis, Mickey, Johnny, Rita, Norma, Bernie, and Mark. I can dream many things, but not a better family.

Rudy Ruettiger

To Carl, James, Jane, and Zachary.
Don't ever grow too old to dream.

Mike Celizic

Table of Contents

Acknowledgments

It is impossible in this brief space to give credit to everyone who contributed to this book. It is literally the product of everyone who has ever helped me to pursue my dreams. It includes all my teachers and professors and tutors at Holy Cross and Notre Dame; my coaches and teammates on the Fighting Irish football team; my friends and associates who encouraged me to pursue my movie; the actors, the technicians, and the dozens of other people who made the movie come to life; and all the people who have come to hear me speak and have encouraged me to put my thoughts down in book form.

But there are some who stand out and deserve individual mention. Among them are: Brother John Driscoll (who has since died), the president of Holy Cross College, and all the brothers and priests of the Holy Cross order; my friend and classmate, Judge Frederico Moreno, Father Jim Reihle, Father Ted Hesburgh, Father Ed Joyce, and Father William Beauchamp of Notre Dame, along with head coaches Ara Parseghian and Dan Devine, and defensive line coach, Joe Yonto; and Merv Johnson and family, Roger Valdiserri, Richard Conklin, and Dennis Moore.

I also want to thank Alan Smith, Andy Heffner, Cheryl and Angie Loverde, Gordon Gillespie, John O'Donnell, Joe Powers, Terry Gannon, Dr. Jack Failla and family, Colonel Jack Stephens, Joe Montana, Bob Golic, Barry Alvarez, John, Don and George Stratigus, Angelo Pizzo, David Anspaugh, Robert Fried, Cary Woods, Alan Mintz, Tri-Star Pictures, Paul Bergan and family, Dennis McGowan, Willie Fry, Bobby Gladieux, Ron Dushney, and Jason Miller.

Finally, my thanks to everyone who made this book possible, including publisher Dr. Wayman Spence, and our editor, Steve Toon, along with Bill Geist, Tom Connor, and Buck Sweeney.

Rudy Ruettiger
South Bend, Indiana

Foreword

by Tommy Lasorda

I get called frequently to give motivational talks. Sometimes, I share the podium with other speakers. That's how I met an extraordinary fellow named Rudy Ruettiger at a speaking engagement.

I liked him right away and I liked his message. We both came from the same working-class background. Neither one of us had anything handed to us. And both of us had pretty big dreams.

He wanted to play for Notre Dame. I wanted to pitch for the Dodgers. We didn't become stars as players, but we played and we didn't quit. I guess you could say we did all right.

I grew up thinking that's what America is about—dreaming, working hard, not quitting, not making excuses. I believed then and believe now that there is an American Dream, and everyone can have a piece of it.

That's what I like about Rudy. He believes in that dream, too. And he knows that you don't get it by making excuses or blaming other people when things go wrong. He's not a whiner. When he gets knocked down, he picks himself up and tries again. He works his tail off and never, ever quits.

We sometimes make the mistake of thinking that all you need to get a job done is great talent. Well, in my business I've seen great talent that couldn't win an intrasquad game. More than great talent, you need great effort. You need the big guns, and you've got to have a lot of Rudy in you, too.

My 1988 World Championship Dodgers were like that. We had to beat the Mets and the A's to win, and nobody said we had a chance against either one of those teams. They had all the stars. We had a bunch of banged-up, gritty guys held together with pine tar and adhesive tape. But we won because that was our dream and because we believed in ourselves.

Managing that 1988 team was like managing twenty-five Rudy's. I've had teams with more talent that haven't performed as well. But the players on that team were as close as any group I've ever seen, and they were willing to do anything it took to win. They wouldn't quit on themselves or on one another.

When I met Rudy on the speaking trail, I thought of the guys on that team. I thought how great it would be if every team could have twenty-five guys with Rudy's spirit and drive.

People ask me what's the secret to success: what's the key to the American Dream? There isn't any secret; no key. You're holding it in your hands.

Just follow the rules—and be a Rudy.

Introduction

I'm okay, you're okay. We all remember that one. It was the fuzzy, feel-good motto of the laid-back generation. Today, it's been remade into a purple, androgynous, nonthreatening, toothless dinosaur named Barney who slides through life on a syrupy slick of "I love you, you love me."

Chill out. Be cool. Don't get upset.

It sounds so good, the kind of thing we want to believe as children; the kind of thing we want our children to believe. But then we grow up and reality hits us in the face like a cream pie. We learn that all good things do not come to those who wait patiently by the fire; that not everyone wants us to succeed.

When we were kids, we used to dream all the time. No one had to teach us to do it. Kids dream like fish swim. We bounced basketballs in the driveway and dreamed about being Oscar Robertson or Wilt Chamberlain or Bob Cousy or Larry Bird or Michael Jordan. Every free throw was with no time left on the clock and the score tied in the seventh game of the NBA championships. Or we played baseball and we were Mickey Mantle or Willie Mays or Reggie Jackson hitting the ball out of the park in the bottom of the ninth. Or maybe we practiced dancing and dreamed of being Fred Astaire or Ginger Rogers or even John Travolta. We dreamed of being writers and singers, doctors and astronauts, presidents and ambassadors.

And then the dreams began to fade. Other people started telling us to get real. These dreams were for others, but not for us. Maybe it was our classmates and maybe it was our parents. Or maybe it was just the way life sometimes seems to make decisions for us.

It was all of those things for me. And it took me a long time to learn that dreams didn't have to die with the end of childhood. They were still there, waiting to be chased down, wrestled to the ground, and made to come true. Yes, I learned, fairy tales do come true, and, yes, it can happen to you. It's tough work. You need determination and energy.

You have to tap everything that's inside you to make it so. But it can be done.

I'm proof of that.

It's easy to look at a Michael Jordan and say, "I can never be like him." But it's just as easy to look at Rudy Ruettiger and say, "Now, *him* I can be like." I'm not smarter than you. I'm not faster, taller, better looking, better dressed, or a slicker talker. I'm five-foot-six and I have the kind of build that will never find its way into an Italian suit. I graduated third in my high school class—not from the top, but from the bottom.

Everyone told me that the most I could dream for was a job in the power plant in Joliet, Illinois. They told me to forget my crazy dream of going to Notre Dame and getting on the football team.

But I got into Notre Dame and I played football.

So then they said I should forget my loony idea of getting a movie made about my life.

But I got the movie. They called it *Rudy*.

After that I wanted to become a motivational speaker, and they said I wasn't smooth enough to do that.

Guess what? I'm a motivational speaker.

And now I'm writing a book to help others get what I have. Some people said I couldn't do that, either.

That's a lot of dreams for one person, but I'm not done. That's something else I learned. You never stop chasing dreams. People ask what made me keep going when everyone told me to give up my dreams and get a real life. The answer is anger.

You have to get mad. And then you have to do it.

Everybody gets mad. It's a river of free energy inside you. It's built into us by nature or God or whatever Creator you choose to believe in. Without anger, humans wouldn't have survived ten minutes in the primeval jungle. It was put there for us to use. But most people don't know how to channel their anger, how to use it to get things done. Instead, they yell or throw things. They punch the walls, kick the dog, abuse the ones they love. They get a headful of rage and take it down to the corner tavern, pull up a stool, and dose it with alcohol, all the while grousing to their beer buddies that life isn't fair.

That's absolutely wrong. It's using your own energy to destroy. And this isn't about destruction. It isn't about hate. It isn't about woulda, coulda, shoulda. It's about living the life you want to live; about achieving your dreams.

It took me a long time to understand that. Somewhere inside, I knew how it worked, because positive anger has gotten me where I am. But we are so conditioned to deny anger, to treat it as evil, that we fight it, stomp it down. And every time we succeed, we don't defeat anger, we defeat ourselves. Well, I've had enough self-defeat to last two lifetimes. And I'm telling you right now it's okay to get mad. Not only is it okay, it's necessary. It got me out of the power plant and into Notre Dame. It got me onto the football team. It got me my movie.

The movie is true. I was a little kid from Illinois with lousy grades and no great athletic talent who decided I wanted to go to the University of Notre Dame and join the football team. I sent in my application and Notre Dame practically laughed in my face. I was too dumb for school and too small and untalented for football. Get real, kid.

I listened to what they told me and I was steaming. It was just like when my father used to get on me as a kid. "Oh, yeah? You think I'm a lazy slob who can't even make my bed right? I'll show you how to make a bed. I'll show you what a clean room looks like."

Later in my life, I thought many times about what he taught me; about how if you're going to do a job, do it right. When I did a job halfway, he let me know in no uncertain terms. But when I did a great job, he gave me credit, told me how well I had done. He's the one who first taught me about not quitting, and the lesson stayed with me.

Yeah, I said those things to myself. And I made that bed and cleaned that room until no one could say I was a lazy slob.

It took me years to get into Notre Dame. I thought I really was dumb until I found out I had dyslexia. I worked in a power plant. I found out what it took to get into Notre

Dame and I did it. I got on the football team. I played. It was only twenty-seven seconds, but I played, darn it. I sacked the quarterback and my teammates carried me off the field. You don't make up stuff like that. It happened.

The story is fairy-tale stuff, but it sure wasn't that way living it. When Notre Dame first rejected me, I was as depressed as a man could get. What was I going to do? Go home to that smelly plant and face the jerks who told me I couldn't make it? Just thinking about it filled me with rage. Forget them. I wouldn't let them beat me down. Not the lunch-bucket bozos and not the lords of Notre Dame.

Anger, you see, gives you courage. Big courage. And when you get courage, you lose the fear of failure.

I went back to Notre Dame and found out what it takes to get there. Then I made a plan for doing it. Finally, I executed the plan.

Once I did that, I didn't have a dream anymore. I had a goal. I wasn't chasing, I was achieving. All I had to do was execute the plan.

Easy? No way.

Doable? Absolutely.

The movie was the same thing. If you think you just walk into a major studio and say, "Give me $14 million. I want to make a movie about myself," you've got another think coming. You bet they laughed at me. You bet I got mad enough to figure out a way to get it done.

I succeeded at Notre Dame because they said I couldn't succeed there. I made a movie for the same reason.

They said, "You're no Paul Hornung or Joe Montana." And they were right. There's only one of them. There's a million of me.

That's why this works. We're all Rudys. The most confident and resourceful and successful people you'll meet are the people who went through a lot of hell to get where they are. Sure, there are the few who are born with silver spoons in their mouths. But most of us don't get spooned. We get forked. That's why this happy-happy, joy-joy stuff doesn't get it done. The real world doesn't work that way.

Let's face it, twenty years after an entire generation declared "Make love, not war," it's still a jungle out there, and most of us enter it on the bottom of the food chain.

You work your buns off, try to be a nice guy, bust your hump to please the bosses, and the next thing you know, you're out on the street. Or somebody else gets the job. Or the people you look up to say, "You can't do that." And when they say it, you look up at the heavens and cry out: "Why me, God?" You had a dream—isn't that what America's supposed to be about, having a dream and chasing it until you catch it?—and now someone is telling you that you can't have it.

And why can't you have it?

Because you're not good enough, that's why. That's what they said.

We all know who *they* are. *They* told me to take up a different major. *They* said I'm too short to play basketball, too slow to play football, too dumb to be a doctor, too homely to get a date with someone attractive.

They've been around forever. Alexander couldn't conquer the world. Columbus couldn't sail west to get to the East. Galileo couldn't say the earth was not the center of the universe. Bill Gates couldn't knock heads with IBM. Lee Iacocca couldn't turn Chrysler around. Evander Holyfield couldn't be heavyweight champion of the world.

Ever wonder what they said to the first cave nerd who sat in the corner rubbing sticks together, wondering if maybe he could make a fire that way? "Hey, Gog. Give it up, you worthless dork. Only the fire god can make fire. Get out there and stab a mastodon. Do something useful."

And maybe Gog got angry when they made fun of him. But before he could do anything, someone told him to chill out. Don't fight them. You can't win.

Can't. Can't. Can't. Can't. CAN'T!

You've heard it. I've heard it. We've believed it, too.

But I'm telling you—don't believe it any longer. They're saying you can't make fire? Damn it. Get mad. Figure it out. Show them who can make fire. You can't climb that mountain that's never been climbed? Says who, you can't?

But you can't sit around and wish it to happen. And you can't spill your anger and hurt on a bar. You've got to turn it to your advantage. It's worked throughout history. Patton used positive anger to win a war. Athletes use it every day to win ballgames. It's the same for a salesman who's told he can't make a sale. I've been there, too. The same for a lawyer who's told he doesn't have a chance of winning that case. The same for all of us. We can sit in our rut and let failure turn to depression. Or we can, as Shakespeare said, "take arms against a sea of troubles, and by opposing, end them."

Yeah, there are a few who have it made. The rest of us are Rudys.

And you know what? Being a Rudy is good enough.

RUDY'S RULE #1

Everyone Can Be Anyone They Want to Be

Successful people know who they are and where they're going. People who fail try to be someone they're not.

For some people, it's easy. Something grabs them early on and they hang onto it without letting go. Maybe they get encouragement from those closest to them, or maybe they're just able to shut out everyone who wants to steer them in a different direction. But, at bottom, they listen early to their instincts.

For the rest of us, it's a long, hard road. We turn a deaf ear to our instincts and try to be what others want us to be. We try to please everyone and find that it's impossible. Failure finds us like a Patriot missile locking onto a SCUD. It was that way for me. It doesn't have to be that way for you.

I am the oldest boy and the third of fourteen children—seven boys and seven girls—in my family. In the movie version of my life, they made my brother Francis—or Frank in the movie—older than I was. That was for dramatic purposes, because they wanted to show me having my fantasies of becoming a great athlete being beaten to death by bigger kids. It was easier than dealing with thirteen siblings in a ninety-minute film. In any event, it was true enough. The fantasies I took into childhood didn't make it to adulthood alive. And I was a runty kid who took endless grief because I thought I was going to be a great athlete. That was going to be my way out, because I didn't see any other way. And there was no other way. That's what I was told. And that's what I believed.

Home was Joliet, Illinois, a gritty, lunch-bucket town an hour or so southwest of Chicago. My dad, Dan Ruettiger, was the sole support of the family. He worked three jobs most of his life to keep our mom and us fed and clothed. His main job was in a refinery, and he worked weekends doing construction and pumping gas at his brother's service station. All seven of the boys slept in bunk beds in a big dormitory room that my dad built onto the house. Growing up, I didn't know that I could be anything I wanted to be. If I ever suspected it, I was talked out of it early on.

I was stupid. That's what they told me, and when you're a kid and adults tell you that, you believe it. You become what people say you are. What they told me was not without reason. I was terrible in school. I know now I have a learning disability; I am dyslexic. But no one knew about that back in the '60s. All they knew was that for me to get a C was a major accomplishment. No one said, "Rudy, you can do better," because they probably didn't think I could. Instead, it was, "Rudy, you better shape up or you're going to get your butt kicked." They looked at me like a clown, so I figured I may as well act like one.

One thing that hasn't changed in forty years is the idea that to be successful as a kid—especially a boy—you have to be a jock. It was true then and it's worse now. Back in the '50s and '60s, they didn't bombard you with ads telling you to be like this superstar or that sweaty hero. But the idea was there.

It's a fast track to failure and disappointment and it's built on the flimsiest of values. Be like Mike, the ad says. And they flash these pictures of Michael Jordan flying through the air, doing impossible things with a basketball. They want kids to think that if they drink the right liquid, they can do those things, too.

There are a lot of things to admire about Michael Jordan. He always stood up both before and after games. He gave everything he had. He worked hard, and he never gave up. Off the court, he helped a lot of people. But the ad doesn't say, be like Mike, work hard. It says, be like Mike, drink this sports drink.

We don't build our kids from the inside, we build from the outside. We tell them to wear this shoe or eat that hamburger or guzzle this soft drink. And when you're on the court, be like Shaquille O'Neil—break the backboard.

The bottom line is we're telling our kids to be like everybody but themselves, and the images we give them are incredibly shallow. Instead of building self-esteem, we make them feel like failures for not being like Mike or Shaquille or whoever the current commercial hero is. There's nothing wrong with dreaming and striving. But we put impossible role models out there. And too often we don't give a kid perspective so that, when failure hits, *they can't deal with it.*

Sports for me were both a blessing and a curse. I wanted to be like Mickey Mantle. The Chicago Cubs and White Sox were the home teams for us, but for some reason I was always a traditionalist. I liked the history and tradition of the classic teams. The White Sox were just another team. But the Yankees—gosh, but that name meant something, just like Notre Dame did in football. They were winners, and that's what I wanted to be.

That's important. You can never lose that desire to be something. No matter what they told me, and no matter how much I believed them intellectually, at some deep-down, gut level, I always thought I was a winner.

I was expected to do great things athletically when I was growing up. Academically I didn't raise any expectations, so it had to be that. And at first, I lived up to what others wanted.

In Little League and then Colt League I was a star. You know the kids who take it more seriously than anyone else and work at it and so become good before the others. That was me. I wanted to make the catch and hit the home run and win the game. I was a little guy, but I would perform.

That's when baseball was my salvation. It got my imagination going, fantasizing about being Mickey Mantle, Tony Kubek, Yogi Berra or Roger Maris. And when I was in Little League and Colt League, my coaches reacted to my enthusiasm. They looked up to me, expected me to do well.

When you get into that situation, it feeds on itself. Because they expected me to do well, I expected the same from myself. It's almost a self-fulfilling prophesy. But I didn't understand what was going on—not then. If I had, it would have made life a lot easier. But I was just a kid, being what people expected me to be.

Colt League is for thirteen- and fourteen-year-olds. I hit my peak there. Then it all fell apart and I fell back into the sucking whirlpool of failure.

I'll never forget it. We were in the playoffs and we were one game away from going to the Colt League World Series. I saw myself going to that World Series, playing in those games, winning, being something. We just had to win one more game.

I was great that day. Every time up I got either a double or a home run. After one of the doubles, I got to third base. We were down one run and I tried to score on a grounder to first and got thrown out. But it was okay. We still had time. In the ninth inning, I got up and got another double. There were two outs, but I thought that we were going to score that run somehow. I thought everybody had the same desire and heart that I did. We couldn't lose.

And the last guy up struck out.

Just like that, my whole dream went away. Poof. Gone. I saw myself in that World Series and I didn't get it. It was devastating. I cried like a baby and felt awful. It was my fault, and I put all the blame on myself. For years, I lived with that. After all, I was supposed to be the star, and I didn't win. I was a failure.

I took it too seriously because athletics were the only thing I had. I was like the kid who thinks he's going to get a scholarship to college for playing ball and when it doesn't happen, he's got nothing else to fall back on. Or the star college kid who dreams about the pros and then doesn't get drafted. You have nothing to fall back on and it's devastating.

Before that game I was a winner—in my head. Now I was a loser and I acted like one. I kept playing baseball, but not like I had before. Just as I had quit in the classroom I quit on the field. Because I quit, my coach treated me like dirt. I got a summer job and didn't put as much time into baseball. My enthusiasm was gone. The coach didn't try to understand or build me back up. He dumped all his anger on me and just beat me to death mentally. My whole identity was wrapped up with being a ballplayer. When that was taken away, I had a serious identity crisis. If I wasn't a great athlete, who was I?

I had no idea.

Oh, I kept playing. In high school, I was a pretty good football player. It was another image of what I wanted to be. Football players were macho, strong, tough. They were like the leading movie hero back then—John Wayne. It's what half the boys in America wanted to be.

But I was five-foot-six-inches, 190 pounds, slow, and played defensive line. Major college football programs don't have much use for people like that, no matter how good they were in a little Catholic high school in Joliet. Some colleges would have ignored a 1.77 grade point average, but only if I were a lot bigger and faster.

But I didn't want to go to just any college. I wanted to go to Notre Dame.

When I was a senior in high school, my class took a retreat at Notre Dame. I had always loved the idea of the school, always dreamed about going there. But Notre Dame wasn't for the likes of me. It was for rich, smart kids; for great athletes. And I was none of those.

But when we went there on retreat, I walked around the campus and was struck by the spirituality of the place. It seemed like home, a place of peace and faith and hope. And the students were like me, the sons and grandsons of European immigrants.

It was then that I first began to know who I was and what I wanted. I was a Notre Dame man. I wanted to go to that school. It made me feel good just being there, better than I had ever felt before anywhere else.

That's how it starts, with an intuitive tremor that strums your spine with a cosmic guitar riff. We've all had those moments when we just knew something was right. But simply knowing isn't good enough, and that leads to another basic truth to reaching your goal:

You must take action to reach the thing you desire.

I didn't act on my knowledge. I couldn't take action, I thought, because I was the only one who thought I could be a Notre Dame man. Everyone else told me it couldn't happen. College was for smart kids. A lunch bucket was for me.

I believed that, just as I believed everything else I had been told about myself. I went back home after the retreat, just barely graduated from high school, and watched all my friends go off to college.

That was an awful feeling. Maybe they had dreams and plans, and maybe they were just along for the ride, but they were going somewhere. I was staying in Joliet. And I couldn't understand why I couldn't have that wonderful feeling I'd had at Notre Dame. The answer, I know now, is because I hadn't prepared myself. That was the action I needed to take, and that is another rule:

Prepare yourself with the knowledge to reach your dream.

I didn't do the work in high school to get into college. I didn't take the courses and get the grades. And nobody else made me see that. So, really, I didn't even know how to prepare myself for that. And now it seemed like it was too late.

In *Rudy,* my movie life, I went to work in a steel mill. In real life, I got a job at Commonwealth Edison—the power plant. It was a good job, something like $12 an hour. You could buy a home and raise a family and retire on that money. Get a job at the electric company, and you never had to worry about being laid off. You were set for life.

To me, it was a sentence, but what was I going to do? I couldn't go to Notre Dame, and when I tried to take a few courses at the local community college and flunked them all, I figured I couldn't go to college at all.

But I wanted to be something more than a factory worker. Don't get me wrong. There's nothing wrong with working in a factory. Pushing a broom is a good and honorable job. I know, because I've done it, and I was darned good at it. But you have to want to do it, and I didn't.

So I talked about how I was going to do something better, and I got put down. My own relatives did a lot of it. There's petty jealousy like that in a lot of families. I talked about doing something different and to them I was trying to be better than they. It was a constant struggle for me to keep going to that job and try to learn to accept it.

I spent four years in that power plant—two two-year terms sandwiched around a stint in the Navy. I had a girlfriend— my high school sweetheart. After work, I'd go to the local tavern with the guys and we'd pound down beers and talk about what we coulda been.

A lot of high school athletes seem to end up doing that. They had that little taste of glory and then it was snatched away. Now they've got this awful job that pays enough to be sort of comfortable, but they're never going to have that thrill of victory again. But they all know they could have been a big deal in college or the pros if only.... The ones who dwell on it too much are sometimes the ones who become alcoholics and slap their wives around, kick the dogs, and hate themselves all of their lives because once they had that glory that's been taken away and they can't figure out how to get it back.

They had memories, but I still had this fantasy about Notre Dame. I would drink my beer and talk about how I was going to go there. Sooner or later, someone would make fun of me or tell me to forget it. I got into a lot of fights that way, because I was carrying a lot of anger and didn't know what to do with it except lash out.

The anger came from the feeling that this was going to be my life. As much as I fantasized about Notre Dame and something better than what I had, I also accepted that this was my fate. And facing that was just awful.

You see, if you're going to decide who and what you are, you have to take control of your life. And I hadn't done that. I let circumstances and others—others who knew what was good for me—take control. I took their word for it that this was the best thing for me. And as long as you permit others to do that, you're always going to be stuck.

My break, if that's what to call it, was the Vietnam War. In time, I would be drafted, no question about it. So, instead of sitting back and waiting for something to happen to me, I decided to take control over how I would serve my military duty.

When I walked into the local Navy recruiting office in 1969, it was the first time I ever took control over my life. That's a rule, one that is critical to mastering your own destiny.

Take control over your life.

I didn't want to be an infantry grunt in the Army, and the Navy had some status attached to it. The uniforms were sharper. More important, you had to take an IQ test to get in. So you couldn't be a dummy and get in the Navy.

I didn't tell anyone when I went to the recruiting office. This was important. If I had told people or asked their advice, they might have talked me out of it. They probably would have tried. By keeping it to myself, I was taking that much more control. I didn't think of it consciously in those terms. At the time, it was more like firing a shotgun up into the clouds because there might be a duck up there. But at least I was doing something, which is a lot better than doing nothing.

It was a personal thing for me. I had to know if I could pass this test and I had to do it by myself. And I have to tell you I was scared stiff before that test. I was used to being told I was dumb, and I didn't know if I could pass it. When I did, it surprised everyone. That was a big triumph and, for the first time as an adult, I had a little self-esteem in the bank. So I went off to basic training very excited. When I got there, I began to learn another truth. And it is this:

If you want to learn who you are, go where nobody knows you.

When I went to boot camp, it was the first time I had ever lived away from home. The old support system was gone, which is a little scary because you're used to it, but is also very liberating, because you don't have to be that person you were.

In basic training, no one knew me from anyone else. We didn't come in with all the labels we had collected back home. The drill sergeants didn't take one look at me and say, "Oh, it's that dumb screw-off Rudy. Forget him." And they didn't look at the guy who was a valedictorian of his class and say, "There's Frank. He's great." We were both treated alike. So the guy who was a local hero and couldn't do anything wrong in his hometown started back at square one, just like me, the guy who couldn't do anything right in my hometown. It was the ultimate level playing field, and in that, I had an advantage, because I was used to being on square one.

In boot camp, you're judged strictly on what you do. Reputations don't count. Effort does. If you perform, you get rewarded.

One thing I could always do was work hard. I had done that in baseball until the coach turned on me. In high school football, I excelled because I outworked everyone. And in the classroom, I was a failure because I assumed I was as dumb as everyone said I was and didn't work at all. At that time in my life, I didn't really understand that yet. But I did know I wasn't going to get dumped on in the Navy because I didn't try hard enough.

Some people just seem to naturally get everything right. They're the ones who have the shiniest brass on their uniforms and the glossiest shine on their shoes. I was never like that. Nothing came naturally, but I could look at how the people who were the best did it and then try to imitate them. So I'd ask the guy who was the best shoe polisher how he did it, and I'd ask the guy with the shiniest brass how he got it that way.

I never thought I'd be the best at any of these things, but I could be part of a group that was the best. And that's how I was perceived; not as the best, but as the guy who tried to be the best. In the Navy, the officers respected me for that.

Maybe some of the other enlistees didn't appreciate my gung-ho attitude. If so, I wasn't aware of them. They were the goof-offs, and I didn't want any part of them. What's more, I didn't care what they thought. In high school, I had been the class clown, and it hadn't gotten me anywhere. Now, I had a second chance and I was going a different route. I was going somewhere, and the way to do it was to do everything as well as I could. My role models in the Navy were the guys who did things the best.

In following them, I was fighting as hard as I could not to be one of the goof-offs. Some people think that those guys are cool. They think it's a triumph if they can get away with doing eight push-ups while everyone else is doing ten. Or if they pull KP, they figure they've beaten the system if they can avoid doing the work they've been assigned to do. To them, the go-getters are the enemy.

Life is full of people like that. They're the cynics, the same people I worked with at the power plant who laughed whenever I talked about getting out of that situation and doing something better with my life.

One reason the goof-offs hate the go-getters is because the enthusiastic guys make them look bad. They're losers, people who have given up before they even start. They don't think of themselves this way, but they're also cowards. They don't want to fail, so they don't even try. It's the old Aesop's fable about the fox and the grapes all over again. When the fox finds he can't jump high enough to get the grapes, instead of figuring out another way to get them, he decides they were sour anyway. Then he probably went back to his fellow foxes and told them how cool he was.

Well, you don't have to be like that fox, and you don't have to be one of the losers. It's not cool to be a cynic. It's *not* cool to be a goof-off.

The problem is that there's a comfort level in being mediocre. Don't try for anything big and you won't be disappointed. You may have the best of intentions and a sterling character, but you can get paralyzed by a decent paycheck. That was true at the power plant. You want to leave, but where are you going to make $12 an hour? You know that there are other things out there that might pay you two or three or ten times as much. And you'd like to do better. But most of us don't know how.

That's where I was before I went in the Navy. I didn't know how to get it. And so I let myself get talked out of it. People said it was impossible to change my life and I believed them. I let the fear of failure paralyze me. So from this I learned another truth:

Don't be afraid to fail.

In the Navy, I began to learn that I wasn't what everyone said I was. Another thing I began to learn is that I wasn't as dumb as I thought I was.

I came out of boot camp as a yeoman and was assigned to a light cruiser in the Maintenance Collection Data Systems Office. This was a job with responsibility and, for the first time in my life, I was perceived as someone who could do something like that. And because others felt that way about me, I felt that way about myself.

When you serve on a ship at sea, you're in a very small, closed society. In that society, the distinctions of rank fade. Everyone has to be able to do every job, and officers and enlisted men worked together in close quarters. I looked up to the officers, and not just the guys with brass on their collars, but also noncommissioned officers. They were successful and, if I wanted to be like them, I needed to know their secrets. So I talked to them as much as I could.

I had discovered mentors in these older and wiser men who took an interest in me and helped me discover who I was and where I was going. For the first time in my life, I had an idea of who Rudy was. These people persuaded me to believe in myself, thus another revelation toward reaching my dream:

Find a mentor who will support you and push you toward your dream.

One officer in particular helped me. His name was Lt. Mark Crowley. What drew me to him was the school ring that he wore. It was a Notre Dame ring.

I asked him if he had gone to Notre Dame and he said he had. I told him I wanted to go there, too, and asked him if he thought I could. The guys I used to hang out with would have laughed at me and told me to get real. But Lieutenant

Crowley said, "Sure, Rudy. You can go there if you really want to."

This was totally new to me. Someone was encouraging me. But he didn't know me as a goof-off who had barely graduated from high school. He knew me as Senior Yeoman Ruettiger, who worked his butt off and did everything he was asked to do as well as he could do it.

I talked so much about Notre Dame with Lieutenant Crowley that when we came into port and had leave, he asked me if I wanted to visit the campus with him. He had a younger brother who was a student there. I leaped at the chance to see the campus again. When we went there, I realized again that I could go there—if I could figure out a way.

The high point of my two-year Navy stint came when they decommissioned our ship, and I was chosen to be part of the four-man crew that shut down the ship. We had to collect all the data in the equipment. It was an important job that had to be done right. And when we got it done, I was the last person off the ship.

That was great, because I had been given a lot of responsibility, more than I had ever had before, and I did the job. That's when I really started to consciously think that I could really go to Notre Dame.

Then the two years were up and I was on the street again in civilian clothes. And all those positive feelings I had came under assault. The reason that happened is because all I had was a fuzzy dream. I still had no game plan.

I found myself back in Joliet and right back where I started—in the Commonwealth Edison power plant. And the same people I had worked with before were there, waiting for me; waiting to start chipping away at whatever good feelings about myself I had developed in the Navy.

God, but that was depressing. All these people are telling me to give it up, that this is my job for the rest of my life, and who did I think I was to think it would be any different. My own father told me to forget about Notre Dame. I don't blame him, though. He was supposed to worry about my having steady employment. And as far as he could see, I wasn't Notre Dame material.

That was still the label I carried. You may as well have scrawled it in big red letters and stapled it to my forehead: "RUDY—Lunch-Bucket Guy."

Our whole society comes down to labels. And that's what we have to change. Because the labels always come down to the positive—the college-bound person—and the negative—the person who's not going to college. If you have that negative label, you're nobody. Don't let other people define what you can and cannot be.

Don't believe the labels others place on you.

We've just gone through twenty years in this country wondering why the Germans and the Japanese could build cars and everything else better than we can. And the reason is so obvious. It's the labels, especially in high school.

Unless you take certain courses, you're labeled a nobody. You have to take those college-prep courses or you're a second-class citizen. And the courses are things like trigonometry and geometry and algebra, where if you don't know how to take the square root of 130 you don't count. No one ever asks what being able to take a square root has to do with being an English major or a history major or a psychology major. Because it doesn't have anything to do with it. If you're going to work for NASA, it means something. Otherwise, who cares?

If you work with your hands, you don't count. This is where Japan and Germany have it all over us. They honor skilled craftsmen. We don't. Instead, kids who go to vocational schools are looked on as losers.

That's garbage. There's no such thing as a dishonorable profession. One great carpenter is worth a dozen paper shufflers in an office somewhere. MBAs are a dime a dozen, but a truly great auto mechanic is a treasure.

So what does this have to do with me?

It goes back to the same attitudes I had to deal with in the power plant. I had a label and it was negative. Just like the college-prep crowd dumped on the vocational-education kids, the factory guys dumped on me because I wanted to go to college. It doesn't matter which side of the blue-collar, white-collar divide you're on. If you want to cross it, you're not going to get encouragement.

I don't care how strong you are, it's tough to deal with. There were periods when I was as depressed as I could get. I thought I was going to be stuck in that plant forever. Like anyone else in that situation, I thought about suicide.

Thinking about it doesn't mean you do it. It just means you've looked down that black hole and wondered what's at the bottom. Even a guy like me, who somewhere inside always thought I could do big things, is going to get to that point. It happens when you keep hitting that wall and can't seem to get through to the other side.

What makes winners is looking down that hole and deciding that you're not going to enter it. Suicide is the ultimate act of a quitter. Athletes who quit when they fall behind, salesmen who quit when times get rough, businessmen who quit when a new product doesn't catch fire right away are all committing acts of suicide. They're not killing themselves, only their dreams.

And that's what pulls you out—the dream, the goal, the hope that you can make it work. All of those things are ingredients of faith. That's something I always had. I was raised on it, and whenever times got rough, it was there to catch me. For me, the belief that there is a God who cares about me makes me care. If God has faith in me, I, too, must share that faith. Even if you're not religious you can have faith. You just have to believe that there is good in the world and that you can be a part of it.

Deep down, I knew I could not quit on life. I was better than that. My faith told me that. And my dreams and hopes

were my road map out. If I kept hitting a wall, maybe there
was a different way to get through it than beating my head
against it. I could climb it or go around it or dig under it.

Deep down I believed that there was something out there
for me. The Navy had confirmed that for me. My friend
Lieutenant Crowley had assured me I could go to Notre Dame.
I wasn't a loser, despite what the bozos at work said. I knew
who I was, now. Or at least who I was working to become.
And I refused to let anyone tell me differently.

Somehow, I was going to get out of there.

RUDY'S RULE #2

Make Anger Work for You

Anger scares us. It scares us so much that there are whole industries dedicated to making it go away. This is the "I'm okay, You're okay" approach.

But sometimes, it's I'm okay, you're an SOB. Sometimes, things happen that tick you off. That's the way life is. It's not all sunshine and light all the time. It's not supposed to be.

And when the clouds roll in and everything and everyone seem to be conspiring against you, you're going to get angry. It's a normal reaction. It's what you do with that anger that's going to make the difference in your life.

I can honestly say that, without anger, I would never have gotten out of that power plant. But at the same time, if I had not learned to use that anger positively, I also never would have gotten out. Anger can make or break you.

In the two years after I got out of the Navy, it almost broke me. If I had been miserable before I went in the service, I was even more so when I got back to Joliet. I had had an initial rush of determination on my discharge. Buoyed by Lieutenant Crowley's encouragement, I had come home and applied to

Notre Dame.

I had no business applying. I hadn't yet done anything to merit admission. But I sent in the application and got rejected out of hand.

This presented problems, because I had told everyone at work I was going to Notre Dame. Before the Navy, I had talked about getting out. I fantasized about Notre Dame. That was annoying enough to my coworkers, but now I was telling them I was absolutely going. I guess it's understandable that they didn't want to hear it.

So they made even more fun of me and I was even more consumed with anger. I released it by getting into fights and going to the taverns and generally engaging in self-destructive behavior.

This is the downside of anger. I could have kept on going that way, talking about what I could have been and what I might have done. I could have married a home-town girl and then come home and treated her like dirt because I was filled with so much rage. I could have had a miserable life.

But I had one good habit. In the Navy, I had learned to seek out positive, supportive people. Back at Commonwealth Edison, I ran into another man like Lieutenant Crowley. His name was Siskel. I owe a lot to that man.

Siskel was probably thirty years older than I. He wasn't a dummy at all. In fact, he was a very bright guy who could have done a lot of things. He used to tell me that he could have been a doctor. But he got out of school and got the job in the power plant and got married and, before he figured out what was happening, he was stuck there. The pay gave him a certain comfort level and he couldn't break out of it.

So now I come along and I'm saying all these things about going to Notre Dame. Siskel listened to me and he didn't laugh at me or insult me. He understood, because he had wanted to do something with his life and he didn't. And now, for him, it was too late.

But it wasn't too late for me. Siskel kept telling me that.

He told me I could find a way to go to Notre Dame; that I shouldn't—and couldn't—give up. Don't make the same mistake he did, he told me.

In encouraging me, Siskel was showing that it wasn't too late for him, either. Maybe he couldn't become a doctor or lawyer because of his family obligations, but he still had great things to do. One of them was to encourage young people like myself.

Everyone has something to offer, but too few recognize that. Siskel did. He had a gift, and the gift was his ability to understand the yearnings of a younger generation and to take them seriously. He could do that because he learned from his own experiences instead of becoming embittered by them. He believed that his station in life did not mean he could never make a difference.

Without Siskel, a man older and wiser than myself, I might have given up. Before I went in the Navy, I had essentially given up once already. After applying and being rejected out of hand after the Navy, I might have given up again. But he kept the flame alive, even if it was only a flicker.

So that should be a lesson for everyone:

Seek out positive and supportive people.

And these are the kinds of people you have to seek out and be around. People like Lieutenant Crowley and Siskel were men who wanted me to succeed. Most everyone else either didn't care or wanted me to fail. If I had hung around with them, I would have failed. Everyone will. But if you go to the people who care, people who are older and wiser, people who know what they're talking about, you can do anything.

Siskel was a good friend. He was a mentor. We ate lunch together and talked about dreams. And then one day, right after one of those lunch-time talks, he died. One minute he was next to me, pumping me up. The next minute he was dead.

In the movie *Rudy*, my friend dies when a steel furnace

backfires. In real life, it happened a little differently, but it wasn't any less sudden or gruesome.

I can tell you what we were eating in our last lunch together. He had his peanut butter sandwich. He always had peanut butter. I had bologna. We ate out of lunch buckets, those American classics with the hinged, domed top that held your thermos. When you had a banana with your lunch, you took the "Chiquita" sticker off the banana and stuck it on the lunch bucket, so after a couple years, the bucket was covered with Chiquita stickers.

When we got done with lunch, there was a problem with the system that fed the coal to the boilers. We'd been having problems with the feeders that shook coal down onto a conveyor belt. There was an electric motor involved that had to be fixed to get the thing running, and that was Siskel's department. My job was to shut the conveyor down so that it wouldn't start up when someone was standing on it working on the feeder.

We snapped our lunch buckets shut and Siskel said he'd go out to the feeder. I told him I'd be right there. I had another job I had to do first. It was only going to take ten minutes.

Instead of waiting for me, Siskel decided he could just jump up on that conveyor and fix the thing. And that's when it started up again. The conveyor vibrates when it runs, and the feeders are only about two feet over it. It threw him right up into the feeder and broke his neck instantly.

I was doing my other job when my radio barked out that there was a problem in the C-1 Tunnel. I knew immediately that was where Siskel was and I ran there as fast as I could. By the time I got the conveyor tripped, he had gone through eight more feeders. I jumped up and started giving him mouth-to-mouth while another guy did CPR on him. When his blood came into my mouth, I felt his neck and knew he was gone.

Hey, people: *Never take a chance with your life.*

When I give motivational talks, I scream this at the

audience. Never take that chance.

A calculated risk is different. Then you know where you're going and you know what's involved. A blind chance is going off without any idea of what's going to happen. That's when you can get killed.

I ask myself all the time why Siskel did it. He'd been on that job a long time and knew better. He probably thought he could just check the feeder real quick and get it going again without anyone else having to be involved. It doesn't matter. He took a chance with his life and he paid with his life.

The ambulance came to collect his body. I stood devastated and helpless under a gray, overcast sky and watched it drive away. And I knew I was out of there.

You see, Siskel was the second good friend I lost. The first died right after high school. Another guy and I were waiting for Ralph at my house. When he got there, we were going to go out. Anyway, he was late, but we didn't think much about it because Ralph was always late. Finally, I called his home and asked, "Where's Ralph?"

There was silence at the other end of the line, and I knew something was terribly wrong.

"Didn't you hear, Rudy?"

"No. What happened?"

"Ralph's dead."

He had been driving over to meet us. Someone swerved into his lane and hit him head on. Ralph, like Siskel, died instantly.

They were both great friends; true friends. They wanted me to succeed. Ralph had been a guy I trusted and hung out with. I viewed him as a kindred spirit—a fellow dreamer. I looked up to him and admired him. When Ralph died, I had asked the eternal questions: Why this? Why now? And there was no answer.

When Siskel died, I felt Ralph's death again, too. And now my reaction was anger. I was mad that they were dead, and outraged that I was still in that power plant after all those years.

As the ambulance was pulling out, I knew that Siskel had

been right. Life is too short not to chase your dreams when you can. I was sick and tired of being that guy who always said I should have been somewhere else; sick and tired of listening to the guys rag my butt; sick and tired of them making fun of me.

For once in my life, the anger pointed me in the right direction. I'm not one of those guys, I told myself, and this time I wasn't just saying it. I meant it. Yeah, I was out of there. Forever. And I'd be damned before I'd go back to that place.

I gave my two-weeks notice and that was that. It was in the fall and classes had already started at Notre Dame. I went up there anyway to find out what I had to do to get in. More on that later.

The bottom line was I had quit the power plant and then learned I had to wait a year before I could begin to try to get into Notre Dame. Those were dark, dark days. I had walked out; told everyone I wasn't going back there. Yeah, you guys. I'm Rudy and I'm going to Notre Dame.

And then I had to wait a year. I couldn't go back to the power plant. There was no way I could listen to those guys again: "Hey, look who's back! What's the matter, Rudy? They don't take dummies up there?"

Again, anger saved me. I went back, all right, but not to the power plant. That would have been surrendering and I wasn't surrendering anymore. I got a job in construction instead and waited out the year. But when that year was over, I was going to be in South Bend. And the reason for doing that was as much because that was my dream as it was that I was going to show those SOBs who made fun of me what I could do.

Anger worked because I had that goal. I knew what I had to do, and the rage drove me toward it. If I had not had that goal, it would have eaten me alive; destroyed me.

So there's another lesson:

Direct your anger toward a goal.

Anyone who says you should never get angry doesn't understand the positive side of anger. They only see the awful destruction anger causes in those who don't have a goal. These are people who have given up. They have nothing to prove; or think they don't. But everyone has something to prove. It's just a matter of finding it.

The power of positive anger can be found almost everywhere that people have been told they can't do something or have had their noses rubbed in their own failures. It's a huge factor in sports, with new stories almost daily about people who have risen up to show that they're better than what the critics say; about overmatched teams that have been embarrassed only to come back and play better than anyone ever thought they could.

From anger comes determination comes triumph, and in sports we see it all the time. It's one of the reasons we find sports so compelling. The drama and emotions take place right in front of us.

It played a huge role in the 1994 Olympic Winter Games from Lillehammer, Norway, the most-watched Olympics in history. And who will ever forget the drama played out in figure skating between Nancy Kerrigan and Tonya Harding?

Kerrigan finished second, losing a gold medal by the tiniest of margins to Oksana Baiul of the Ukraine. But that wasn't the story. And it wasn't the way that Harding fell apart during the competition and Kerrigan skated the program of her life, either.

The real story was how Kerrigan dealt with the horrible events leading up to the Olympics.

Before the United States Figure Skating Championships in January 1994, Nancy Kerrigan was known as a beautiful and talented skater who somehow was never able to come up big at crunch time. Just the same, she was a co-favorite at the national championships with Tonya Harding, a tough, athletic skater from Oregon. The top two skaters in the competition would go to the Olympics.

Not satisfied with Harding's chances, her on-again, off-again husband, Jeff Gillooly got together with her bodyguard and two other bozos to guarantee a Harding victory. Together, they conspired to whack Kerrigan on the right knee after a practice session just before the championships. The lasting memory of the attack was Kerrigan sitting on the floor, holding her damaged knee, sobbing hysterically, "Why me? Why me?"

No one who saw that could fail to identify with Kerrigan's anguish. She had worked for her Olympic moment for most of her life and now she was sitting on a cement floor, not knowing if her leg was broken, and there was no answer to that awful question. It's what I felt when my friends died. It's what you've felt when catastrophe has struck.

Within a week, when the plot unraveled, Kerrigan—and the world—knew why her. She and Harding immediately became the center of a media feeding frenzy the likes of which has seldom been seen. And what everybody asked her as she recovered and began skating again was, how would she do in the Olympics?

The pressure on an Olympic figure skater is enormous under the most ideal circumstances. It is only once every four years, during the Olympics, that the world takes figure skating seriously. Win at the Olympics, and fame, glory, and a whole lot of money are yours. Fail and you spend your days dressed as a chipmunk in the chorus line of an ice show. The routines are enormously difficult and demanding. The odds are on the side of failure.

But Kerrigan was now thrust into an even fiercer spotlight by the attack. Worse, she had to live in the same building with Harding and share the same practice ice with her. The two hadn't been friends before the attack. After, Kerrigan couldn't help but wonder if Harding had been involved in the attempt to end her career.

Kerrigan said all the right things in public and did all the right things. The public saw her smiling and saying sweet nothings to the reporters and thought that she was a fragile flower; a "nice girl." But she is from just outside Boston and has a blue-collar background. This woman was as tough as nails.

Inside her tightly knit support group, the real Nancy Kerrigan was fuming. She had every right to be mad. Some nut had tried to derail her dreams with a steel rod to the knee. Now, when she should have been concentrating on skating, she was in a traveling sideshow. She had to put up with the constant presence of Harding.

Her response was to use her anger to prove to everyone that Nancy Kerrigan, who had wilted before under ordinary pressure, could triumph under the most extraordinary pressure any skater had ever faced. She skated the best long program of her life. Brought the sold-out arena to its feet. Burned her image of triumph into the soul of everyone who saw her perform.

She didn't get the gold. Figure skating judging took care of that. But she won anyway because she overcame not only circumstances but herself. She got mad and she did it. And no matter what happened after that, Nancy Kerrigan has that triumph forever.

How about the U.S. Olympic Ski Team? Going into Lillehammer, the team was savaged in the media. *Sports Illustrated* wrote that all the people and half the cows in Austria and Switzerland could ski faster than U.S. racers. The skiers could have felt sorry for themselves, but they didn't. They got mad and took golds in the biggest races of them all—the men's and women's downhills. And with every medal and every success, they talked about those who had written them off. The message was never said in so many words, but it was clear enough: "We showed you."

Players always complain when the newspapers write about how badly they're doing. But coaches love it. Players who are mad at the media are players with something to prove.

In 1986, the New York Giants won their first Super Bowl.

The man who led them offensively was quarterback Phil Simms. Since being drafted by the Giants in 1979, Simms had done a lot of things right, but he had been injured often and he had also made some big mistakes to lose important ballgames.

By 1986, Giants fans were booing Simms' every mistake and the media were debating whether he should be the Giants' starting quarterback. A prominent New York writer said in print that the Giants would never even get to the Super Bowl much less win it with Phil Simms as quarterback.

Simms held his tongue, but inside he was seething. When the Giants finally got to Pasadena to play the Denver Broncos in the big game, someone asked Simms about all the criticism he had taken. "All those people who said the Giants would never get to the Super Bowl with Phil Simms as quarterback can kiss my grits," Simms fired back. Only he didn't say "grits." He said that Tuesday. Five days later, with the world watching, he had the greatest passing day in Super Bowl history and led the Giants to victory.

Chalk up another win for productive anger.

Bill Parcells, Simms' coach through two Giants' Super Bowl triumphs, was a master at manipulating both his players and the New York media. He convinced his players that the writers were their enemies. Then he pointed out his team's shortcomings to the writers. When they wrote what he told them, the players were only more convinced that the writers were out to get them. All the way to their second Super Bowl win in 1991, the players celebrated every victory by reminding the writers that, "You guys picked us to finish fourth."

Some players are naturally motivated. But in the course of a long season, most get complacent at one time or another. The press is just one of the weapons coaches use to regain the edge that winning teams have to have. A man like Bill Parcells worked his locker room constantly, needling players about their shortcomings, telling them about how the big monsters on the other side of the line were going to eat them alive. It didn't matter who the player was or how great he was. Parcells used the same tricks on Lawrence Taylor, one of the greatest players to ever pull on pads.

Parcells made his players mad. He put them in that "I'll show you!" state of mind. Some of Taylor's greatest games came after Parcells spent all week making him mad.

It's the oldest trick in the book. After one particularly dreadful half of football against an inferior team, Knute Rockne, the legendary Notre Dame coach and master motivator, let his team sit alone in the locker room for the entire halftime break. Finally, just before they were to go back on the field, Rockne appeared and gave a three-word speech in tones dripping with sarcasm: "Let's go, girls." Thus stung, an angry Notre Dame team went back on the field and destroyed the enemy.

Bobby Knight catches a lot of flak as the irascible coach of the Indiana basketball team. But there's a method to his madness. Many of his tricks are aimed at making his players mad enough to play their best. He doesn't worry about being politically correct, which is the same as not letting others dictate to him. The bottom line is his kids turn out to be great team players as well as contributors to society. John Thompson at Georgetown, John Cheney at Temple, P.J. Carlesimo at Seton Hall, and hundreds of others work the same way. And nearly every year their teams excel.

When I was the last man on the depth chart at Notre Dame, I didn't need coaches to make me mad. Every day I went out at practice and I was a human tackling dummy. Getting beat to a pulp every day gave me all the anger I needed.

My anger made me resolve to figure out a way to make the varsity work harder. Being a pushover wasn't helping anyone, and if I had sat back and just let them walk all over me, I wouldn't have lasted a week. Those monsters would have broken me into a million pieces. As it was, they beat me up badly. That was their job. My job was to take the lumps willingly, to help the team to get better. But I didn't have to take it with a smile. And I didn't. Getting mad made me think of ways to beat those guys. It gave me the strength and determination to fight back.

After getting worked over, I'd sit up thinking about it. On the way to practice the next day, my mind was going a hundred miles an hour: "Dammit! What do I have to do to keep from getting my butt kicked again? Dammit. Those SOBs are going to kick my butt again. I gotta think of something."

And the anger would make me think of something: "I got it. I'll get lower. I'll make those big suckers work. They're not going to get me."

Of course, it worked both ways. Because when I went out and made them work harder and made them look bad, that made them mad at me. They'd try yelling at me: "Rudy! You're making me look bad. Why don't you ease up?" Maybe they'd take a swipe at me.

That's the kick-the-dog stage of anger, except I was the dog. It doesn't work, though. I was still making them look bad. So they'd have to use that anger to beat me legitimately. You notice, the bottom line is the same—Rudy gets smashed. But we're all doing it at a higher level. And because of that, the guys who had to work against me were better football players; they were more ready to play on Saturday.

As much as they cursed me, they knew that. After a while, they thanked me. They knew that if I hadn't worked so hard and made them mad enough to really put out, they wouldn't have been as good as they were.

If I had just gone out and coasted, they might have liked me better, especially at the start. I would have been good-old-Rudy, the guy who made them look good. But I didn't want to be that guy, and because I refused to play that role, I became something better. And the guys who didn't like me when I started respected me in the end.

Let me tell you. I tried it both ways, and being respected beats being liked.

I was just the last guy on the end of the bench. But it works that way for teams, too. In 1992, Boston College came out to Notre Dame for a football game and got the tar kicked out of them. Big-time teams like Notre Dame beat up on other teams all the time. But this game was a special beating. Notre Dame not only won, they ran up the score. Leading by something like thirty points, Notre Dame coach Lou Holtz called for a fake punt. He got a first down out of it and eventually yet another touchdown.

That play was the last straw for Boston College. The Eagles could handle getting beat, even beat badly. But running a fake punt when you're winning big is rubbing it in. Boston College couldn't do anything about it that day, but they didn't forget.

A year later, the Eagles came back to Notre Dame. The Irish were undefeated and looking at a national championship. All they had to do was beat Boston College. Under ordinary circumstances, they would have won easily. But these weren't ordinary circumstances. All week going into the game, the Boston College players thought about how Notre Dame had embarrassed them the year before. They thought about how Notre Dame had run up the score.

You think the Boston College coaches told their players, "Now, men, don't think about last year. Don't get mad at those guys. It's not nice to be angry?"

No way. They just grabbed onto that anger and made sure the players channeled it into winning. When the game was over, Boston College had its revenge. And Notre Dame had lost its shot at the national championship.

It was hard to find anyone who felt sorry for the Irish— outside of South Bend, anyway. From the beginning of time, bullies have been sowing the seeds of their own destruction. Notre Dame knows that as well as anyone. Some of the Irish's greatest wins have been fueled by the anger generated from horrible losses in the past. Every team knows it, yet they keep doing the same thing. And sooner or later, it comes back to defeat them. It does because it ticks people off.

The patriots who started the American Revolution were moved to action because the British ticked them off. The French Revolution caught fire because the ruling aristocrats ticked off the common man. The American labor movement began because workers had taken enough and weren't going to take any more.

Anger was the fuel. What happened then depended on a goal—on leadership.

I talk a lot about anger. It's only part of the puzzle, but it's an important part. And so often, especially in a team setting, another part of the puzzle is love.

The two go hand-in-hand, just like in a family. Some people make fun of teams that talk of themselves as families, but some people make fun of everything. Don't listen to them. They're losers and they want you to lose, too. Because teams that win are families. When one member suffers, they all suffer. Their anger comes from the love they feel for one another.

I really saw this at work during the 1993 college football season when Barry Alvarez, a former coach at Notre Dame, asked me to talk to his new team, the University of Wisconsin Badgers.

Barry is an extraordinary man, especially among coaches. When he was offered the Wisconsin job, most of his friends told him not to take it. Wisconsin was a loser. Other Big Ten teams began their seasons by looking at the schedule, finding the Wisconsin game, and putting a "W"—for Win—next to it. The top high school prospects didn't go to Wisconsin. The second-best prospects didn't go there, either. They went to the big schools with histories of success.

Besides not having any players, Wisconsin didn't have any money, either. When Barry ignored everyone's advice and took the job, the program was millions in the red. The booster club—the source of extra funding for big schools—didn't even have a hundred active members.

Barry took the job because he had a vision of what could be done. He didn't care that he didn't have the greatest prospects to work with. When he picked his assistant coaches, he didn't drill them on X's and O's—the technology of the game. Every coach knows about X's and O's. What Barry wanted were assistants who cared about kids. If a prospective assistant talked about kids and how he loved working with them and wanted to make a difference in their lives, that was the man Barry wanted.

He told his kids right off he knew they were at Wisconsin because the traditional powers didn't want them. And he told them they were special, because even though they couldn't get into one of those big schools, they wanted to play. They had heart and desire. And if they had that, they could be something.

By 1993, he had a group of seniors who had been through four years with him. They had started like every other Wisconsin team; by getting beat up, by getting laughed at. But they believed in each other and they didn't give up. Slowly, they got better. Slowly, they started winning football games.

And now that they were seniors, they were fighting mighty Ohio State for the Big Ten Championship and a trip to the Rose Bowl. The week before that game, Barry asked me to come up to Wisconsin and talk to his team.

They watched the movie *Rudy* first. Then they gathered everyone together—sixty players and a dozen coaches and administrators—and Barry introduced me.

I have to confess. I never know exactly what I'm going to tell a group I'm speaking to. I have to see them first, feel their energy, try to understand what they need. And as I'm waiting for Barry to introduce me, I'm thinking, "What am I going to tell these guys? They know this is the biggest game of their lives. They know why they're here."

So this is what I told them:

"Look, I'm not standing in front of you to hype you for Ohio State. You don't need that. You know why you're here because you put yourselves here. You did it. You picked yourselves up by your bootstraps. You're the ones who were 1–10 three years ago. And you're the ones who decided to be better than that.

"That's the greatest advantage any human being has—to make that decision whether or not you're going to make it happen for you. What happened five minutes ago doesn't matter. What matters is what happens right now.

"That's what's great. You can do anything you want. Right now. Just by making that decision."

I looked at these guys who had been through so much together, and I saw the togetherness in that room. And I talked about that, too.

"I've been watching you guys for two days now," I told them. "And I feel a lot of love in this room. There's a lot of love here. It's how you look at each other, how you respect each other. Don't be afraid to say that to each other. Don't be afraid of that."

Then I gave them something else to think about. "I feel a lot of anger in this room, too," I said. "You guys have been pushed around enough. You're angry. That's okay. You guys should be mad. I want you to get mad. You're mad because of what they said to you, that you were nobodies. You're mad because you were the second and third choice at all these other schools.

"You guys took all that anger and you channeled it in a positive way. You created a team. You created unity."

They went out against Ohio State and they played their butts off. But they made some mistakes and they didn't win. Ohio State didn't win either; it was a tie. Afterwards, the players were pretty down. One who came up to me and asked for my autograph looked pretty apologetic for the outcome, so I told him, "Number one, you didn't lose this football game. Number two, you weren't even supposed to be out there competing with Ohio State. And number three, Ohio State could lose next week. You guys still have a shot at the Rose Bowl.

"Don't give up. Don't ever quit."

They looked at what they did wrong that caused that tie. Then they went out and won the rest of their games. Ohio State lost. And Wisconsin went to the Rose Bowl, where they won again.

Now that's the way to use anger. Not out of hate but out of love. Not to lose, but to win.

RUDY'S RULE #3

Everyone Should Dream

Everybody can dream. Everybody.

Columbus had a dream. Alexander the Great had a dream. Thomas Edison had a new dream every morning. Martin Luther King Jr. had a dream. George Washington, Abraham Lincoln, John F. Kennedy, Bill Clinton—they all had dreams. I don't care who you name. If they did something in this world, it started with a dream.

You've got a dream, too. Maybe a lot of dreams. When the movie *Rudy* came out, a lot of teachers took their students to see it. I got a lot of letters from those kids, and most of them told me what an inspiration the movie was. But a few were different. One boy wrote to tell me he didn't like the movie. He said he was "lame" and could never be a football player, and so the movie didn't relate to him.

That letter broke my heart. Someone had so convinced that kid that he couldn't do anything that he couldn't see what *Rudy* was all about. It didn't have anything to do with being a football player. It was about chasing a dream. Going to Notre Dame and playing football—even for twenty-seven seconds— was my dream. Your dream can be anything. Being physically challenged can't stop you from dreaming.

Dreams don't have to be glamorous. Maybe your dream is to drive a cross-country truck. Maybe it's to make furniture. Maybe it's to be an animal trainer, an undersea explorer, a football star, a real estate king. Maybe it's just to own a special stamp or coin.

When I worked as a finance insurance salesman for an automobile dealer, we had a kid who washed the cars in the lot. Richard was an inner-city kid with a high school education, and he took the job because he needed to make a living.

He had a stuttering problem, but he didn't let that stop him from dreaming. He used to tell me he wanted to be a salesman in the showroom, and he'd ask me how he could do that. I told him he wasn't ready yet, but if he worked hard, he could earn the right to be one. "What have you done?" I'd ask him. "Show me you deserve to be a salesman."

It's not hard to get a job washing cars in a lot. It's something else to use that as a steppingstone to something better. That's what Richard did. No one did a better job getting a car ready for a customer than Richard. It wasn't long before every salesman was asking him to get their cars ready.

When he wasn't washing cars, Richard hung out around the salesmen. He learned everything he could about selling cars, and then he learned everything he could about every other area of the business. The last time I saw him, he was twenty-two years old and he'd succeeded beyond his dreams. Instead of selling cars, he was the finance and insurance manager for a major dealership.

What I'm saying is your dream could be anything. I don't know what it is. But I know you have it.

I also know if you're like me, you've spent your life listening to people telling you to stop dreaming. If I had a nickel for every time an adult—parents, teachers, aunts, uncles, you name it—told me when I was a kid to quit daydreaming, I could buy General Motors.

I listened to those people. But I didn't listen all the way.

Oh, I listened enough to forget about going to Notre Dame right out of high school. I listened enough to get that job at the power plant. But I never listened all the way. Some part of me always held on to the shredded end of my dream and wouldn't let go. And that's what saved me.

America is built on dreams. How many times do you read about people who caught the American Dream? A lot, right? But how many times do you say to yourself, "That could be me?" Not as many, right?

Don't kid yourself. We sit around saying, "I wish that were me," instead of "That could be me." And then we sit back and grouse about the American Dream. It's a lie, we say. It's for other people.

And that's where we're wrong. The American Dream exists. It's out there for everyone. But it doesn't automatically come just with being an American. It starts with building castles in the air and then with knowing the difference between a fantasy and a dream and finally with making it come true. But it starts not with what is, but with what could be.

Colonel Sanders, the chicken king, had a dream. He had a recipe for chicken that he knew people would buy. Only no one would listen to him. He drove all over the South cooking his chicken and getting sent on his way. But he kept at it because this was his dream. Finally, he made it come true.

Ray Kroc had a dream. He was the man who founded McDonald's. When he bought his first restaurant, all he wanted to do was sell milkshake machines. But the key was, he dreamed about selling a lot of them, and the way he saw it happening was to start these fast-food restaurants where they sold a whole lot of shakes. The dream didn't quite lead to milkshake machines, but that's how dreams go. You start in one place and you end up in another, and sometimes that other place is better.

The point is, dreams aren't just for the other guy. They're for everybody. As kids, we can't stop dreaming. It's what life's about. But as we grow older, we let others convince us that there are certain things we can't do. We get discouraged when everything doesn't work right away. We get caught up with earning a living, with getting by. At first we put our dreams on hold. And there they gradually fade until we don't think we can reach them. We give up.

And some of us regret it all our lives. In our spare time, we tell everyone about all the things we could have done, how we could have as much money as that guy, or we could have been the boss, or how we could have played for the Yankees or the Celtics or the Dallas Cowboys. But we didn't.

Look at Michael Jordan, the greatest basketball player of all time. He retired at the peak of his career. He'd reached all his goals, attained all his basketball dreams, he said. He wanted to try something else.

Nobody believed him. He'll be back, they said. He's too competitive, they said. He'll get tired playing golf, they said.

And then Jordan shocked everyone. He said he had a new dream—to play major-league baseball. And that's what he was going to try to do.

Now, people either laughed at him or criticized him for trying to do what couldn't be done. He hadn't played baseball since high school. Baseball requires a lifetime of practice to play on the major-league level. He'd never hit a curve. *Sports Illustrated* devoted a cover to telling him to quit before he embarrassed himself and the game.

That's ridiculous. Michael Jordan had a dream and he was given the opportunity to pursue it. He earned that opportunity with all he did on the basketball court. He didn't care if the White Sox were giving him a tryout as a publicity stunt. What mattered was that he had the chance.

"I've never been afraid to fail," Jordan said during spring training. "That's something you have to deal with. I think I'm strong enough as a person to accept failing, but I can't accept not trying."

Here is the real reason you should want to be like Mike:

You can't succeed if you never try.

And that's what it's all about. Because if you don't try, you go through life bitter and full of regret. When that's the alternative, your only choice is to dig down and find that dream that's still inside you, drag it out of the grave you put it in, breathe life into it, make it real.

Before you do that, you have to answer a question:

Is it a dream or a fantasy?

When I was a kid screwing around in school and daydreaming about Notre Dame, I didn't have a true dream. I had no idea if it could happen, no plan for getting there. Notre Dame was a fuzzy, feel-good fantasy. I didn't really think I could go there, because I thought Notre Dame was for kids who were rich and brilliant. I was neither of those.

All dreams start that way—as fantasy. The kid shooting baskets in his driveway, pretending he's Shaquille O'Neil, is engaging in a fantasy. It can't be a dream because becoming the next Shaquille O'Neil requires more than wishing it so. You've got to be big and strong and a great athlete, and no kid will know if he'll be any of those things until he grows up.

The kid who fantasizes about just becoming an NBA player is a little closer to reality. But that's a stretch, too. It's too far away with too many unknowns.

It's not what I call a possibility dream.

That doesn't mean it can't happen. It just means that when you're ten years old, you don't yet know enough. But that doesn't mean that all dreams are fantasies.

A fantasy is beyond the realm of possibility. A kid fantasizes about being Shaquille O'Neil, but he doesn't yet know if he'll be five-foot-ten or seven-foot-two. Only when he grows up can he know whether that fantasy becomes a dream. A dream, then, is something that is possible. The key in evaluating fantasies is to understand whether they are impossible because of real factors, or because you won't make them possible. You don't just sit down and say, "I can't do that." You have to weigh all the factors. When you do, you may find that parts of your fantasy can be real; can be attainable dreams.

That same kid who fantasizes about the NBA can also dream about making his elementary school team. That's a dream he can see; a dream that can be realized by almost any normal kid who's willing to work hard enough to get there. Then he can dream about making the junior varsity team, and then the high school varsity team, and then playing in college.

Michael Jordan's basketball career started that way. He dreamt about making his high school team. And the first year he tried out, he didn't make it. He could have quit right there, but there was nothing physical holding him back from that dream. He kept working and made the team the next year. But that was his first dream—to make the high school team.

For some of us, that first dream may not be possible. What we have to do then is adjust our dream so that it is possible. If you don't have the talent to make the team, you can still be a part of it by becoming a team manager. You can get to the National Basketball Association that way—and have a much longer career than a player.

The point is if your fantasy is to be in the NBA, it may not be possibility dreaming to try to get there as a player. But it's possible for anyone to become involved in the NBA in some way. If that's what your dream is.

Reality—or what we think is reality—is the enemy of fantasies but not of dreams. Maybe you dreamed as a kid of becoming a fighter pilot, but then you had to get glasses. You have to have perfect vision to be a fighter pilot. But that doesn't mean you can't have a dream. You can work on the flight crew. You can design fighter planes. You can build them or program the computers. There are dozens of ways to be involved with fighter planes that don't involve actually flying them.

But you have to be careful about reality. It's not what others say it is, but what you discover it to be. Take me and my boyhood dream of going to Notre Dame. As I said, I thought it was a fantasy. That's what everyone told me.

But then, when I was a senior in high school, I went there. The Catholic school I went to sponsored a retreat at the seminary across the lake from the campus. Naturally, as soon as I got there, I went to the Notre Dame campus and walked around. The students I saw were just like me. They weren't all rich kids or geniuses with their heads in the clouds. They were regular guys. And right then, my fantasy got a little closer to being a dream.

What made it a dream is that once I saw the campus, I was able to begin to visualize myself being there. I had never actually seen myself at Notre Dame before, and that's why going there had been a fantasy. But now I could see myself walking the campus with my books under my arm, a Notre Dame jacket on my back. In my mind's eye, I didn't look out of place. The students I saw looked just like me. Okay, I didn't have the grades they did, but I'd figure that part out later. The breakthrough was when I could begin to visualize. That's when the fantasy started to become a tangible dream.

Visualize yourself living your dream until you believe it to be real.

So if you don't know if you have a dream or a fantasy, try to visualize yourself in the position you want to be in. If you want to be that fighter pilot and you have bad eyes, the vision doesn't fit. It's a fantasy. But you'll be surprised how real your fantasy can be.

It took me ten more years to get to Notre Dame, but that first trip there began to show me it might be possible. The reality I had imagined was not the way it really was. So that's another rule:

Don't believe everything you hear. Find out yourself.

Years later, I discovered just how right Notre Dame was for a dreamer like me. The school was founded by a dreamer.

When people think of Notre Dame, they think of Knute Rockne, Paul Hornung, Rick Mirer—football heroes. But the true spirit of the school comes down directly from its founder, Father Edward Sorin, a French missionary of the Congregation of Holy Cross.

In 1842, Father Sorin and a small band of missionaries arrived at the south bend of the St. Joseph River and founded a school. It was supposed to be a place where the farmers who were then settling what was still the frontier could send their sons for basic education. But Sorin saw more than a frontier school in his first log cabin. Where others saw near wilderness, he saw a great university.

He didn't have any money, but that never bothered him. True dreamers are like that. They don't let anything get in their way. Sorin was willing to do anything to finance his school. He even sent a contingent of priests to California to join the gold rush of 1849. They came back empty-handed, but at least they tried.

The priests made the bricks for the original buildings with their own hands from the mud at the bottom of St. Joseph's and St. Mary's lakes that were part of the tract he purchased. And he didn't build a puny, little frontier school building. He constructed a great building of the yellow bricks.

And then disaster struck. Sorin's first building—the whole school—burned to the ground. He had no money and now he had no school. Sorin and his priests walked through the still-smoldering ashes, and as his comrades wept, Sorin dreamed.

He said, "Our Lady's mad at us, because we dreamed too small. We have to dream bigger."

The other priests couldn't believe what they were hearing. Their dreams were in ashes, but their leaders' dreams had barely been singed. "Yes," he repeated. "We didn't build big enough. This time, we'll rebuild and the new building will be as great as our patroness, the Virgin Mary. And on top of the building, we'll put a great dome and we'll gild it in gold."

They didn't have money for bread and Sorin was talking

about gold. And somehow, they built that great building and they put a golden dome on it. It's still there; the Golden Dome that once was the entire university and now is the heart and soul of the great university that Sorin dreamed of.

And on top of the dome is Our Lady—Notre Dame—with her hands spread out overlooking the campus and overlooking all the dreamers who come there, because Notre Dame is a land of dreams. It's where dreams come true.

When we were working to make the movie *Rudy* come true, we had to get Notre Dame's permission to film on campus. This wasn't as easy as it sounds. The last time Hollywood had brought their cameras on the Notre Dame campus had been before World War II, when Pat O'Brien and Ronald Reagan starred in *Knute Rockne, All American*. In the fifty years since, the school jealously guarded its image, and rather than have that image tarnished, it refused all requests to make another movie there. For the administration to change that policy was going to take a lot of convincing.

I won them over by telling them about Father Sorin and about dreamers. Over the years, the public had come to see Notre Dame as a football factory; a university interested only in how much money it would make on its next TV contract. I pointed that out and talked about how that isn't what Notre Dame is about at all. It's about people like myself; people who dream not about becoming a professional football star but about just walking on that campus, looking at the Lady on the dome, becoming some small part of the tradition there. And they saw that. I made them dreamers, too.

Father William Beauchamp, Notre Dame's vice president, is the man who made the decision to let us make *Rudy*. He deserves enormous credit, because he did one of the most difficult things for anyone. He changed.

It's called flexibility. Successful people are flexible people. They are willing to listen to new ideas. It doesn't mean they are wishy-washy and jump on every bandwagon that passes by. Father Beauchamp is anything but that. Rather, he is a man of conviction and strong belief. But he was willing to listen to what I had to say. When presented with compelling arguments, he was willing to change.

The easiest thing in the world is to keep doing what you've always done. It's why my friend Siskel was still working at the power plant twenty-five years after he started there. He could have done something different. But he couldn't bring himself to change. The dream was there, but he wouldn't listen to it.

So here's another rule for making dreams come true:

Change is necessary.

We deal with change constantly. And we deal with it in a negative or positive way. Maybe we get a new boss, and we don't understand where the boss is coming from. That's a change we have to deal with.

How many people do you know who confront a change like that and see only the negative? You've probably done it yourself. You get together on coffee breaks and complain about how the new boss has changed everything. It's not like it used to be. Everything is new.

You do that and all you get is miserable.

It doesn't have to be that way. If we're going to win, we have to look at change as a positive thing. We have to take it and make it positive. Sure, it upsets our routines, but it also presents us with opportunity. Too often we don't see it that way because we focus on how it affects us instead of the opportunities it opens up for everyone involved. A star quarterback can look at a new coach and complain that his job is going to be changed. Or he can look at it as an opportunity for the whole team to be more successful. When we look at the bigger picture and don't worry about how much credit we get individually, everyone prospers. From change can come victory.

Whatever happened yesterday happened. It's over. History.

What's happening now and what's happening tomorrow is what's important. And it all depends on how we deal with change.

It's up to you this very second to forget about what happened five minutes ago. Right now you can change your whole life. Right now you can change your whole perspective, your whole vision. Right now is when you start making your dreams come true.

So view that new boss as an opportunity. Go in and ask him or her what you can do to make things work. That boss has a dream, too. If you can help him or her make that dream come true, it can help your own dreams. It's a chance to start fresh, and maybe get that promotion you've been dreaming of. But if you take it as a negative "Oh, heck. What's this new guy going to want? We were doing fine the way we were."—you're not going anywhere.

Things happen when there's change. Whether it changes for good or bad is up to you.

Father Beauchamp was willing to change, and it came out pretty good for Notre Dame. *Rudy* countered all the cynics who look down at Notre Dame or any place with ideals. It showed that the school is about a lot more than Heisman Trophies and pro football stars.

And it started with a change.

I'm not saying you have to change everything right now. You don't have to quit your job, because there's nothing wrong with any job. There's nothing wrong with working in a factory. It wasn't right for me, but it may be for you.

But I am saying that if you're not happy, get out. Change.

And to do that, you have to stop listening to what others tell you. You have to listen to yourself; believe in your dreams. No one else is going to believe in those dreams if you don't believe in them yourself. They'll try to talk you out of your dreams, and if you buy into that, you'll be just like me when I was working in the power plant, letting everyone tell me I wasn't going anywhere, especially to Notre Dame.

That's the biggest change you can make in your life—to stop buying into what people say you're supposed to be, instead of being what you want to be. That's when the tide turns. That's when you start to do extraordinary things.

Jim Valvano, the basketball coach and broadcaster who died of cancer, used to say that ordinary people do extraordinary things every day. It happens when they stop doing things because of the perceptions of others, but simply do them to the best of their ability. That's when work—and the worker—acquires dignity; when it's done as well as you can do it. Maybe you feel you can't forge big changes in your life, but you can do that much. You can do everything you undertake just as well as you can.

The thing to remember is that extraordinary depends on the individual. For a kid with great grades, going to Notre Dame isn't extraordinary. For me, it was. It was something I dreamed about but thought I'd never do. And the reason I didn't think I would is because I listened to others. Once I listened to myself, it became possible.

That's why *Rudy* had such a big impact on people who saw it. Going to Notre Dame was extraordinary for me. I conquered the battle with low self-esteem, and as I learned to believe in myself, my personality grew stronger; I like myself more. It's why I'm asked to travel around the country to talk to people with dreams.

People can relate to me in ways they can't relate to a Joe Montana. There's only one Joe Montana, but there are millions of Rudys. I'm not tall and slim and movie-idol handsome. I'm short and square and I look like a guy who used to work in a power plant in Joliet, Illinois. And I don't talk like an English professor. My grammar isn't perfect and I lisp a little, but I don't worry about that. It's not important unless you let it be.

I go places now, like to the auto dealer to get an oil change, and the secretaries come up to me and say, "Rudy, I really feel better about myself after seeing what you've done. I know

I'm better. Seeing your movie made me feel better about myself."

These are people I ran into before the movie. Maybe they thought I was nuts when I was running around the country, spending every nickel I had trying to get a movie made about my life. I don't know. But now, when I see them, they're dressed better, they groom themselves better. Maybe they've lost some weight. It's just little things, but they show that these people have hope now. Because they saw what I did and they know I'm not smarter or better looking or more talented than they are.

Before they saw the movie, they bought into it when people told them, "You're never going to be anything more than a secretary." And now they've got hope. They're starting to believe they can have dreams; that they can change.

This is another thing about dreams. It's never too late to start making them come true. My own brother, Frank, is proof of that. Like me, Frank didn't go to college right out of high school. Instead, he went to work in a factory. But that wasn't what he wanted to do with his life. His dream was to become a policeman.

But the paycheck and all the doubts kept him at the factory. For thirteen years he stuck to that job.

I always told Frank, "Be what you want to be. If you're not meant for college, who cares? That's not you. What do you want to do?"

And he said he wanted to be a cop.

"Dammit, then go do it," I'd tell him.

"I'm not smart enough," he argued.

"The hell you're not. You can do it. Get your butt in there. You'll find a way. I found a way. You can, too."

It took Frank thirteen years, but he finally did it. He went down and got on the list to take the police test. When that happened, they sent him to the University of Illinois to take courses to be a cop.

Frank was like me. He never studied in his life. Going to college after all those years was scary for him. I told him,

"Frank, I was in the same boat. You get help and study harder than anybody. You'll make it because this is what you want. Even if you only pass by by one point, you'll be a better cop because of it. Believe me."

Frank went to college and studied for the first time in his life. He worked his butt off there, and when they took their tests, he just barely passed, but he did pass. He got his badge and today he's one of the better cops you'll find. He's good because he enjoys the work. He enjoys helping people. It's what he always dreamed of doing.

So you have to go after what you feel. You have to be who you are and who you want to be. The road isn't always going to be paved. But nobody said it was going to be easy. It's not supposed to be easy. If it were, everybody would be the person they fantasize being. They wouldn't have to turn fantasy into dream into reality.

And you know what? It wouldn't mean anything. It would be like reaching for the remote control, pushing a button, and changing the channel. Dreams don't come true by pushing a button. Make that another rule:

To dream is to risk.

I stressed that late in 1993 when I was asked to come to the Peach Bowl to talk at the pre-game banquet. The teams that would play in the game—Clemson and Kentucky—were the guests of honor at the dinner. My speech was for them.

"Look," I began, "not too many years ago I was sitting at my high school graduation wondering what the heck I was going to do. I was a nobody. And ten years later I graduated from Notre Dame. Now what made that happen? Here I was sitting there with a 1.77 grade point average, number three in my class—not from the top, but the bottom.

"I went to work in a factory, went through all these changes in my personality and, all of a sudden, I go on this journey. I take this risk. Notre Dame was really where I wanted to be, and it happened. But how?

"I wouldn't let anyone take it away from me. That's how it happened.

"And that's where you're at. You're in a position in your life to be in a football game that a lot of kids want to be in. But they're not here. You are.

"A lot of us take that for granted. But the people who really respect where they are and don't take it for granted are the kids who are going to do well in that game tomorrow. They're going to play their butts off. Because they know they only get a shot like this once in their lives. And when you get that shot, you have to go for it.

"And that's what we do in our lives. We position ourselves and once we get in that position we don't let anyone take it away from us. That's where I was. Once I put myself on that edge, I wouldn't let go. Sometimes it's good to put yourself on that edge. It makes us do things. That's what it's about.

"Take that risk. Take that challenge."

And then I told them the story about the Wisconsin players who were rejects from other schools. They went 1–10 their first year under Barry Alvarez, and then 5–6 and then 6–5.

And all the while Barry told them they could be better than that; they could be somebody.

They believed and they started dreaming about winning the Big Ten and getting that one chance to play in the Rose Bowl. They believed because Barry believed what he was telling them. They started expecting success. And when they put themselves in a position to go to the Rose Bowl, they didn't let go. They played their butts off.

Wisconsin won their Rose Bowl, and Clemson and Kentucky went out and played maybe the best Peach Bowl ever. They all laid everything they had on the line. They had their one chance, and they didn't waste it. Dreams are precious things, and when you come within sight of yours, you can't let it go.

It starts with a dream. We have to plan how we're going

to get there and then work hard to execute that plan. We have to be flexible enough along the way so that we're not afraid to change; to seize opportunities as they arrive.

And it ends with achievement. That's what life is all about.

RUDY'S
RULE
#4

Eliminate the Confusion

4

Okay, you've decided who you really are. You've turned your anger in a positive direction and used it as motivation. You've defined your dream.

Now what?

That's the question that stopped me from going to Notre Dame for six years. I knew I wanted to go, but I didn't know how to get there. I had no plan.

Dreams are tough that way. They don't come with owners' manuals or road maps. And, if they're big enough, they look impossible to get to. It's like setting out to build a house without knowing anything about construction. What do you do first? Where do you get the materials? What kind of hammer do you need? What size nails? How do you make the pipes stick together without leaking? How do you do the wiring?

You look at all that and your head starts to swim. All you see are obstacles. It's like giving a five-year-old a three-thousand-piece jigsaw puzzle. He sees all those tiny pieces and starts to cry. The sheer size and complexity scares him, and he ends up quitting before he starts.

If I had looked at my movie like that, it would never have

been made. I mean, how do you get Hollywood to make a movie about you? Wow! It's too much, too big. You can't just walk into a studio president's office and say, "Hi! I want to make a movie. It's about my school days. And I'll need $14 million to make it."

So you can't do that; you can't look at the enormity of what you want to do. At least you can't look at it all at once. It will scare you to death. You'll either be afraid to fail or afraid you'll actually succeed. Don't underestimate the second fear, either. Fear of success is a mighty enemy. It's one thing to dream, but it's something else to actually attain it. What are you going to do with it when you get it?

It becomes very important, then, to visualize exactly what you want to be, and only that. That's your first key. If you can visualize what you want to be and eliminate the confusion and fears, that's when you start getting places.

Book stores are full of volumes telling you how to plan your life. You can read them forever and maybe they'll help and maybe they'll just convince you it's just too complicated. It's like that jigsaw puzzle. Try to understand the solution all at once, and you won't get anywhere. But if you start with the corners and the borders, and then do the big features, pretty soon you've got it done.

So sometimes it's best not to know a whole lot before you start. Sometimes you've just got to go do it. Otherwise, the confusion overwhelms you.

Believe me, if I had looked at everything it took to get a movie made, *Rudy* never would have made it to the big screen. Heck, if I had known everything I would have to go through to get to Notre Dame and then to play twenty-seven seconds with the Irish varsity, I'd still be in that power plant. But I didn't know anything. All I knew is what I wanted to be. And when I knew that, I went and did it.

There is really only one thing you have to know before you set out: That it can happen. After that, take on each obstacle as it comes. And never, never, never look for obstacles. Believe me, they'll find you all by themselves. Worrying about them before they appear won't help at all. Sometimes, worrying about obstacles only serves to create them.

Maybe you're thinking right now that this sounds too simple. There's got to be more to planning. What about all these other books I read with all these clever guidelines? What about them?

Well, I never claimed to be clever. I'm a simple guy. I'm not good at fancy talk and charts and graphs. But I've achieved my dreams. And I've done it because I never thought of why it couldn't happen. I've done it by being too dumb to make it complicated.

I've talked about how my friend, Siskel, died on the job, and how that convinced me I had to get out of that factory. The anger I felt both at the loss and at the prospect of spending my life there swept away all the doubts I had. At that moment, I was going to Notre Dame. I made that decision, and that's what I did.

I drove up to the campus. I knew that Father Hesburgh, the university president, lived in Corby Hall, so that's where I went. It was late when I got there, but I knocked on the door. Father Hesburgh wasn't there, but Father Cavanaugh, who had been the previous president, was. I guess I didn't make a lot of sense at first, because he thought I wanted to become a priest, and he wasn't sure that was a good idea. I finally explained that I wanted to become a student.

I knew I wasn't going to get right in. My grades weren't good enough, and besides, the term had already started. But I had come up to the campus before to see a football game, and on the way I passed Holy Cross College, which adjoins the Notre Dame campus. I had realized that maybe that was the way to get to where I wanted to go. And Father Cavanaugh told me that Holy Cross, which was a junior college affiliated with Notre Dame, was where people like me could go to try to get into Notre Dame. That's where I could get the grades to enter and show I could do the work.

I had to go back to Joliet and work construction for the rest of the year, but I had taken the first step. I eliminated my fear and I went there.

That's often as much initial planning as you need. What it lacked in detail it made up for in simplicity. If I had sat down and said, Well, I have to get an appointment with Father Cavanaugh, get into Holy Cross, rustle up money for tuition, take a lot of courses that I'm not going to understand, get straight A's for two years, and then hope I make it to Notre Dame, I might never have gone to South Bend. It's that puzzle again. It's too big.

But driving up there and knocking on doors until I found somebody who would talk to me was easy. Any fool can do that. Heck, even a Rudy can do that. And that's a lesson that Mao Tse-tung taught his followers a long time ago:

A journey of a thousand miles begins with a single step.

It's been said in other ways. K.I.S.S.—Keep It Simple, Stupid. Don't sweat the small stuff. We'll cross that bridge when we come to it.

What's simple is different to different people. There are a lot of intelligent people who can look at something I can't make heads or tails of and put it right together. That's terrific. But the thing to remember is it's not complicated to them.

You can't worry about how somebody else does something. You have to take your own path. But no matter how bright you are, keeping it simple—for you—is the key.

When you keep it simple, you can't get confused. When it's simple, nothing can stop you. It's when you start to complicate things or when you get around people who want to complicate things for you that doubt sets in and you stop.

That's how I got into Notre Dame. Father Cavanaugh kept it simple. The first thing I had to do was go to Holy Cross. He could see how important it was to me and how sincere I was, and he saw to it that I got in.

For all those years in the power plant, I listened to people who told me how it was impossible for me to get into Notre Dame. They told me all this stuff and I listened to them. I made the same mistake later in life, after I graduated from college, when I was working for an insurance company and thought that I could be president of the company. But everyone told me I couldn't do it. There was too much to know. And I believed them. I thought you had to know every aspect of the business, every policy, every clause, all the fine print. I couldn't do that. It was too confusing and I quit.

In reality, I could have been president of that company, because it's not about knowing all those details. It's about people. What's there to understand about that? The employees know what they're doing. You've got people working for you who can do the teaching and the understanding. The president's job is to motivate them; to orchestrate the show. It's like building that house. So what if you don't know how to do it yourself? You just assemble your team of plumbers, electricians, carpenters, masons, and painters. Then you motivate them to do the best job they can do. That's your job.

When you look at it that way, a funny thing happens. All of a sudden, just by being there, you start to understand how it all works. One of the jobs I had in the power plant was as pump room operator. The first time I looked at all those pumps and gauges, I freaked. "Holy cow! I'll never be able to do this. If something goes wrong, the whole place is going to blow up! There's no way I can ever be the guy to run this thing. It's too complicated."

But I didn't have to run it all right away. I learned what one gauge meant and what one valve did. Anybody could do that. And when I learned one, I learned another, and another, and pretty soon that pump room wasn't complicated at all. I made it simple by keeping it simple.

Where we go wrong is when we jump around instead of concentrating on one thing at a time. And when you accomplish that one thing, congratulate yourself. Don't think about all the other things you didn't do, or all the things you don't understand. If you do, you end up right back where you started. But if you focus just on that one good thing you did, all the things you don't know don't mean anything, because you'll overcome them, too. One at a time. What you're doing then is breaking your big goal into a lot of little goals.

So there's another rule of planning:

Have a new goal every day.

And make that goal something you know you can do. You can't sell a house every single day if you're a real estate salesman. But you can get a listing, or make ten phone calls, or rewrite an ad, update your files, or even just get your car washed. Then, at the end of the day, you don't have to sit down and say, "What am I going to do? I didn't sell a house." You have something that you did, something positive that will help you make those sales down the line.

It's not all going to be roses. Nothing worth having is easy. But if you take things one at a time, it will happen.

My big dream was to get on the Notre Dame football team and put on the uniform. Not to be a starter for the varsity. That was unrealistic. But to just put on that uniform on a Saturday morning, stand in that tunnel under the stands with that wonderful, green, grass field ahead of me surrounded by walls of screaming people, and then to run out there and be a part of that wonderful tradition. That was the dream. But I wasn't even in Notre Dame yet. And I wouldn't get in if I didn't take care of the small goals that would get me there.

When I finally entered Holy Cross, my goal was to get an A average. That was the only way I was going to get into Notre Dame. I had never gotten a B before, so that was a big goal. But I also figured it was a goal that could be met with hard work. And because I wanted it so badly, I didn't mind that.

I threw myself at the books for the first time in my life.

After a few weeks of class, we had our first set of quizzes. I got F's on every one.

It was devastating. I had worked my tail off and I was still flunking everything. If I had been at a lot of other schools, no one would have cared. But at Holy Cross, people did. Brother John, my advisor, knew how important this was to me and how hard I was working. When he saw what happened, he knew there must be a reason. He had me checked for learning disabilities and we learned that I am dyslexic. No wonder I had never done well in school. When I read something, I don't see it correctly.

You can't cure dyslexia, but you can deal with it. For me, it meant that I had to read everything several times before I had it right. Brother John, the other teachers, and my classmates helped me in other ways. They taught me how to take notes, how to study, how to write. They weren't like the guys in the power plant, who wanted me to fail. And I didn't fail. Once I knew what was wrong, my grades started to go up immediately.

There's another lesson:

Surround yourself with people who want you to succeed.

Boy, but that's so important. A lot of people look at what I've done, and they say, "Man, that Rudy's an incredible pest! Showing up on people's doorsteps in the middle of the night. Always pestering them about his dreams. Gung-ho and rah-rah all the time."

And to them I am a pest. But it's funny, because Father Cavanaugh didn't think I was a pest. Brother John didn't think I was a pest. Lieutenant Crowley didn't think I was a pest. My friend Siskel didn't think I was a pest. The executives at Tri-Star Pictures didn't think I was a pest.

The difference was these people wanted me to succeed. They set me up for success and encouraged me. When I needed help, they saw that I got it. Without them, I never would have gotten anywhere.

I got my A's that first year. Both semesters. That's what I had to do, and with all those people helping me, I did it.

They had told me that I had to get A's for four semesters—two full years—before I could get into Notre Dame. I thought that since I got A's for two semesters, I could get in. I talked to Brother John about it all the time, and he told me the same thing—I had to do another year.

I went against his advice and applied anyway. When the rejection letter came, I cried, just like in the movie. I went back to Brother John and asked him if there was something I hadn't done. He told me I was doing everything I could do. I just had to do it again.

So I did it. And this time I got in. The first part of my dream was a reality. I didn't have any money other than what I was getting from the G.I. Bill. But I wasn't going to let that stop me. When you're chasing a dream, you don't let anything stop you. I found out that Notre Dame would give me free board in a room in the Joyce Athletic and Convocation Center—the athletic arena. I didn't have a dorm life—although I did have a roommate, Pete Murphy—but I had someplace to live. I could handle the rest.

Now, I had to get on the football team.

You have to remember, I'm eight years older than the freshmen going out for the team and four years older than the seniors. I'm five-foot-six, 190 pounds, and slow. This is not the prototypical Notre Dame football player.

But I was living my dream now, and I didn't care about that. As soon as I got into Holy Cross, I had gone to see Ara Parseghian, the head coach. Just walked into his office, because that's the simplest way. He couldn't figure out what was going on or who I was. He told me then I couldn't try out for the team because they had already been practicing for several weeks. I told him I wasn't going to try out that year, but the next year.

I did other things to become part of the campus. While I was at Holy Cross, I spent a lot of time at Notre Dame. I even held office in student government and took part in the Bengal Bouts, Notre Dame's annual amateur boxing tournament. I wasn't supposed to do any of that. I wasn't a student there. But that's how badly I wanted it.

When I finally got my chance, I put everything I had into the two-week tryout they had for walk-ons, which is what they call nonscholarship players. Nobody pretends the walk-ons are there for any reason other than to be human blocking and tackling dummies for the big boys. But a football team needs a lot of guys like that for practice, and they have to be good and tough or the team isn't going to be able to prepare for big-time opponents.

After the first day of tryouts, I came into the locker room feeling like I'd been run over by a dump truck. I went to the trainer, and he said, "No wonder you hurt. You have your pads on backwards!" That's how excited I had been. I hadn't even noticed.

I made the practice squad over better players because I wanted it more and I worked harder than anyone. It didn't mean enough to them. It meant everything to me. And I'm not just talking dreams, here. If I was on the team, it meant I could eat at the training table. With my financial situation, if I didn't have that, I couldn't eat at all. So I was out there not just to fill a dream, but also my stomach.

All the time, my ultimate goal was still to dress for a varsity game. But if I looked at it like that, I never would have made it. The gap was too big. There were like a hundred guys on the team, but the National Collegiate Athletic Association allowed the team to dress only sixty players for games. A lot of guys would never get to put on a uniform.

So I broke it down into small goals. To be respected, you had to get gold football pants to wear at practice. The absolute scrubs wore white pants. I wanted the gold pants. Once I got those, I wanted to get into the main locker room instead of the spare locker rooms that the scrubs dressed in. Sometimes, I helped myself. Like getting on the depth chart. That was another goal. Every football team has a depth chart. It's posted in the locker room and it's a big board with every position listed and then the players listed underneath with the varsity on top, the second string under him, and so on. I was so far down the list that I wasn't on the chart, not even as sixth team.

I could have waited forever to get on the chart and not made it. I just wasn't important enough. So one day I went up when no one was around and wrote my name on the depth chart—at the bottom. From then on, it stayed there. I'd go up to fifth string now and then, but mostly I was at the bottom— sixth team. But at least I was on the team. I existed. And like the gold pants and the locker room, that was a status thing.

It's like that in many jobs. How do you become a radio personality? An anchorman? A columnist? Businessman?

You do it by getting in the door. Which door you get in doesn't matter. I got into Notre Dame and onto the football team through the back doors. The important thing was I got in. You have to go to that place you want to be, knock on the door, and ask. Don't worry about whether anyone will talk to you. You'll find someone who will. Believe it or not, most successful people want to help others be successful. They can tell if you want something badly enough to really work for it. They'll tell you how to get there, just like Father Cavanaugh and Brother John told me.

And don't worry about what job you get to start. The important thing is getting in the door. If you have to start in the mail room, do it, and be the best person they've ever had. And while you're doing that, learn everything you can about how the business runs so that when a promotion comes open, you'll be there to fill it.

People still get to the top of important businesses by starting in the mail room. Radio talk show hosts start by being gofers. Newspaper columnists start as news clerks—the modern equivalent of copy boys and girls. Remember my friend, who had only a high school education and stuttered, who started in the auto business by washing cars and became a finance and insurance manager?

When people call me up now and ask me, "Rudy, I have a great movie idea. How do I get somebody to make it?" I tell them what I can, but I also tell them, "Just do it!"

If you really, really believe in your dream, you'll get there. But you have to have passion and total commitment to make it happen.

When you have passion and commitment, you don't need a complex plan. Your plan is your life is your dream. So that's another rule of planning:

Decide what you want to do, then do it!

That will get you started. But no one can reach a dream on their own. I know that, and it's why I love watching the winners come up for the Oscars and Emmys. They don't come up, grab the statue, and say, "Boy, I'm good and I deserve this." Instead, they thank all the people who helped them get it. Successful athletes say the same thing. Michael Jordan gets the MVP trophy in the playoffs and he says, "I couldn't have done it without my teammates." Great running backs and quarterbacks say, "My blockers deserve this as much as I do." They take their offensive linemen out for dinner, buy them expensive watches, even give them cash. The fans might think Emmitt Smith does it totally on his own, but Smith himself knows better.

Life isn't any different than sports. You can't win without a good team. While athletes can sometimes pick their teams, they can't pick their teammates. But you can. That's a huge advantage you have in making your dreams come true.

Things started to change for me when I stopped listening to people who didn't share my dream and started associating with people who wanted me to succeed. Lieutenant Crowley, Siskel, Father Cavanaugh, Brother John, and all my other friends weren't just advisors. They were my teammates. They helped me, and I helped them. Brother John's dream, for example, was to help people get into Notre Dame and make something of themselves. By helping me fulfill my dream, he was fulfilling his own.

That's how I attained my second big dream—to make the movie *Rudy*. I assembled a team of people whose dreams coincided with my own. Together, we made them all come true.

People come up to me and look at what I've done, and say, "Wow, Rudy. You sure are lucky." Yeah. I'm lucky, all right. All it took to get *Rudy* to the big screen was three scripts, a couple of lost jobs, every penny I had, six years, and several of the biggest selling jobs of my life. Yes sir, I sure am lucky.

The movie wasn't even my idea—at least not originally. It started when I was invited to some local Notre Dame Alumni Club meetings to talk about my adventures getting into school, making the football team, and playing twenty-seven seconds in the last home game of my career. After several of these talks, people came up to me and told me, "That's a great story, Rudy. You ought to make a movie." We've probably all said that at one time or another about some story we've heard. But that's as far as it goes. But the more I thought about it, the more I liked it. I had been kicking around from job to job after graduating from Notre Dame. I was successful at all of them, but none of them aroused that passion in me that my quest to go to Notre Dame and make the football team had. I had become like everyone else—a guy trying to make a living, without the dream that makes everything come alive.

The movie idea changed all that. It gave me another dream to chase. But how do you make a movie?

I didn't have the faintest idea. But I knew I wanted to do it. That had been enough to get me to Notre Dame, why not to Hollywood?

All I knew was that if you wanted to make a movie, you had to have a script. So a friend of mine and I sat down and wrote a script. It wasn't a very good script, but that wasn't important right then. At least it was a start.

You could make a pretty good comedy about our first attempts with that script. After we wrote it, we decided we needed to have an agent. I was living in Baltimore at the time, and we knew that a lot of agents worked in New York. So my friend and I got a couple hundred dollars together and went up to New York to find an agent.

We no sooner arrived in New York than we came across somebody running a three-card Monte game on a street corner. Three-card Monte is the modern equivalent of the old shell game. Except instead of looking for a pea under a nut shell, you look for a certain card. It looks simple, especially to hicks like us. That's how it's supposed to look. Otherwise, the scam artist wouldn't have gotten every penny we had. Which ended our trip to New York.

It went like that for several more years. I ran into someone else who knew someone who was a professional writer. I met him and he agreed to write another script. He moved into my apartment to work. Then he brought his girlfriend in, and she started the kitchen on fire. When I finally threw them out, he took my credit cards with him. In return, he left a gigantic phone bill.

But he also had written another script. Rather than lose my dream, I let him go, because he did have some Hollywood connections. He agreed to continue to try to sell the script. What I didn't know is that he put his own name on it and took mine off.

A lot of people would have quit by then. But I don't believe in quitting on dreams. And I knew the problem wasn't the script. It was getting the right team together. So far, I hadn't done that.

Finally, I got another break. I was talking to a friend in a hotel lobby in South Bend about how I had to get a good writer when the hotel manager interrupted me. His name was John Stratigus, and said he couldn't help but overhear me. His brother, Don Stratigus, knew a screenwriter by the name of Angelo Pizzo. Angelo had written the hit movie *Hoosiers*, about an Indiana high school basketball team from the boondocks that beats the big-city school to win the state championship. John thought maybe his brother could help me get in touch with Angelo.

It was a lucky break, but it wasn't really luck. I could have told John to get lost. I could have gone through that lobby without talking about my movie. But I didn't. And that's another key. You have to stay open to people and ideas. You don't brush someone off because you don't think they're important. Everyone is important. And if you operate that way, you meet people and make connections. Businessmen call it networking. I just say this:

You can never know too many people.

Good people make good things happen.

Through Don, I got in touch with Angelo and told him my story. He told me straight out, "Rudy, I'm sure it's a fine story, but I have to tell you two things about myself. One, I'm never going to do another Indiana sports movie. Two, I hate Notre Dame."

I didn't argue with him, but I didn't give up, either. I knew that Angelo was perfect for my movie. I just had to convince him of that. I did that by finding out what his dreams were and then helping him to fulfill them.

Hoosiers was Angelo's first major motion picture. It was also his last. He continued to write successfully for television, but he wanted to write another movie script. He'd tried different projects and ideas, but nothing worked like *Hoosiers* had.

I let some time go by and I called him again and asked him to have lunch with me. He agreed, but warned me that he wasn't going to do it. I had another appointment that morning, with Jake Steinfeld, the "Body By Jake" guy. He had expressed interest in the movie, but when I met with him, he didn't want to listen to how I wanted to do it. He had his own ideas, which included himself playing Rudy. He also thought he could market his own business through the movie.

Sometimes, that's the way it goes. You get someone who's interested, but not in the same things you are. Your dreams don't mesh. The temptation can be great to go with it, especially if you're inexperienced. But you only have one shot at a dream, and I don't think it's worth selling it out.

After leaving that meeting, I went to the restaurant where I was supposed to meet Angelo. I sat, and sat, and sat, drinking coffee, getting more anxious as Angelo didn't show. Finally, I got up, paid the bill, and went outside. I was frantic. Angelo was the perfect man to write *Rudy*, and I had to find him.

I had no idea where Angelo lived, but I went out into the neighborhood, thinking somehow I would find his house. When I saw a mailman, I stopped him and, in desperation, poured out my story. The mailman said he wasn't supposed to give out addresses, but he must have been impressed by my story. And he must have felt sorry for me, because he told me how to find Angelo's house.

I thanked him, found the house, and knocked on the door. Angelo, who had forgotten all about the meeting, answered it in his bathrobe. I introduced myself, and he said, "Rudy, you're even crazier than they say." My reputation must have gotten around.

We had our meeting, and I pointed out to him that his dream was to write another movie. He'd tried other projects and, for whatever reason, they didn't work out. Maybe this wasn't his ultimate project, but he had to get another movie out to let people know he was still around. And I understood his feelings about sports movies and Notre Dame, but by vowing never to do another movie like *Hoosiers,* was he ignoring that maybe this is what he does best?

I told him a lot of other things. He said he'd think about it. When he had, he agreed that I was right. He would write the screenplay for *Rudy*.

Through Angelo, we got David Anspaugh, the director of

Hoosiers, to direct *Rudy*. David hadn't directed a successful movie since *Hoosiers,* and he, like Angelo, could fulfill his dream of another major motion picture through my dream. Other people fell into place. Finally, I had my team.

If I had it to do over again—and I do dream of making another movie—it would be easier. But now I know who to go to. I know people, and I know the system.

In effect, I've learned how to run that pump room at the power plant. If I'd looked ahead for all the obstacles I eventually ran into, I never would have started. But I started by ignoring the negatives and focusing on what I could do. Little by little, it came together. The cost was enormous in time, money, and emotions. But it was worth every bit of it.

RUDY'S RULE
#5

It Is Better to Do Something and Fail Than to Do Nothing and Succeed

5

People who say they've never failed aren't trying hard enough; they aren't dreaming big enough. They've found a comfort zone in life and they're not going for greatness. They're not even going for the next level. Right where they are is safe and predictable. Why mess it up?

Well, for a lot of those people, there is no reason to change. We need people who have found a comfort zone; need a lot of them. There's nothing wrong with being comfortable as long as it's for the right reasons.

If you don't take risks and don't fail because you're satisfied with life, that's fine. But chances are, if you're reading this book, you're not satisfied. Maybe your life is running smoothly, but deep down, you feel trapped in what to you is mediocrity. You'd like to do something else. You have dreams. But you're afraid.

Fear comes in two basic forms: fear of failure, and fear of success. I've talked about fear of success a little. It's really the fear of the responsibilities that will come when you reach your goal. Like maybe you want to be the next Michael

Jordan, but you're afraid that if you get there, you'll have to be a great role model, you'll have to deal with tremendous media attention, you'll be expected to make the game-winning shot every night. Or maybe you want to be president of the company, but if you get there, you subconsciously fear the social obligations, the enormous responsibility of making personnel decisions, or any and all of a hundred things.

But right now, I want to talk about the fear of failure. That's the fear I had to confront. When the lunch-bucket brigade told me I couldn't get into Notre Dame, I was afraid they were right; that I'd fail and have to come back and listen to them laugh at me.

Once I got mad enough to ignore the fear, I found out that it's not worth worrying about. I had thought that it's bad to fail.

I found out it's not bad to fail. It's good. In fact, it's necessary. You learn from failure.

You learn to win by losing.

And that's what I tell people in my motivational speeches. I'm not here because of success. I'm here because of failure and what I learned from it.

I failed at my studies all through high school. I failed at my first try to get into Notre Dame. I failed hundreds of times on the football practice field, and got my butt kicked good because of it. I failed and failed and failed again with my movie. I had ten jobs in my life and got fired from five of them. The others I quit.

I learned from every one of those failures. My failure to get into Notre Dame taught me to work harder. My job failures taught me about what I really wanted to do. My football failures prepared me for my one chance to play in a real game.

In the movie *Rudy,* I get into the football game on the kick coverage team with twenty-seven seconds left. After the other team gets the football, I have one actual play and on that

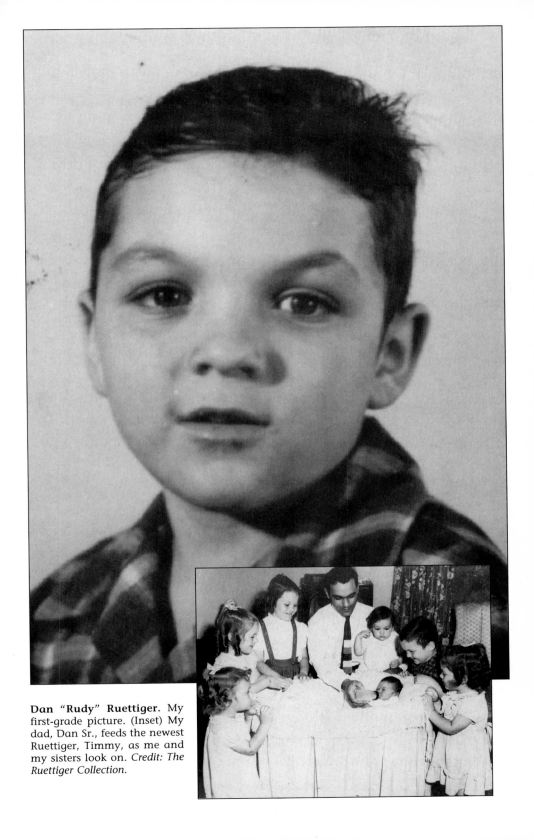

Dan "Rudy" Ruettiger. My first-grade picture. (Inset) My dad, Dan Sr., feeds the newest Ruettiger, Timmy, as me and my sisters look on. *Credit: The Ruettiger Collection.*

First communion at nine years old. (Inset) First place in the Catholic Youth Organization eighth-grade basketball tournament. *Credit: The Ruettiger Collection.*

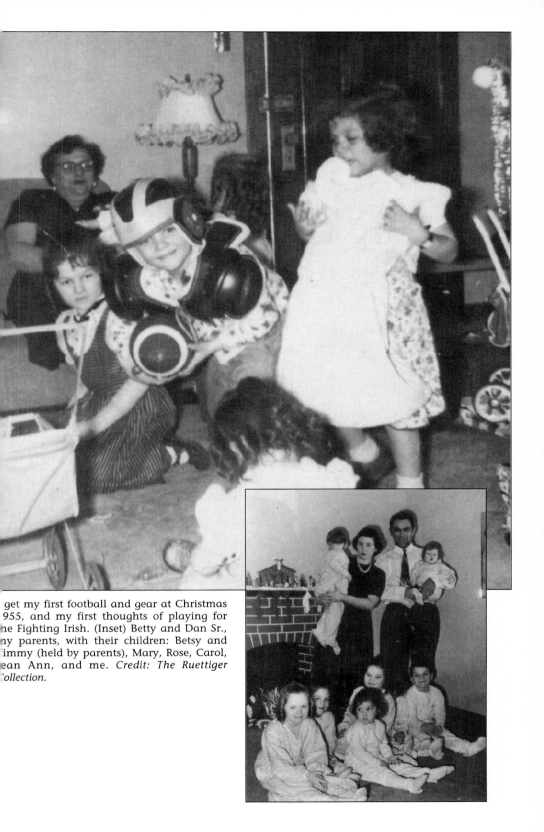

get my first football and gear at Christmas 955, and my first thoughts of playing for he Fighting Irish. (Inset) Betty and Dan Sr., ny parents, with their children: Betsy and immy (held by parents), Mary, Rose, Carol, ean Ann, and me. *Credit: The Ruettiger* ollection.

All of the Ruettiger kids: Top (l–r) — Rose, Betsy, Carol, Mary, and me; Bottom — John, Tim, Berni, Mick, Norma, Jean Ann, Rita, and Francis. Not pictured: Mark. *Credit: The Ruettiger Collection.*

Despite being small, I excelled in football in high school for the Joliet Catholic Hilltoppers. I'm No. 65 in the bottom row in the team photo. My friend, Ralph (No. 69) is in the lower left. (Above) A touchdown-saving tackle. *Credit: The Joliet Catholic Hilltopper, 1966.*

I had a passion for all sports, particularly baseball. These are my teammates my senior year in hig school. *Credit: The Joliet Catholic Hilltopper, 1966.*

Me at bat. Team sports taught me about competition and sticking to a goal. *Credit: The Joliet Catholic Hilltopper, 1966.*

My best friend, Ralph Girot, was killed in a car accident. *Credit: The Joliet Catholic Hilltopper, 1966.*

Graduating third in my class in high school—third from the bottom. At this point no one, including myself, believed I could ever reach my dream of going to Notre Dame. *Credit: The Joliet Catholic Hilltopper, 1966.*

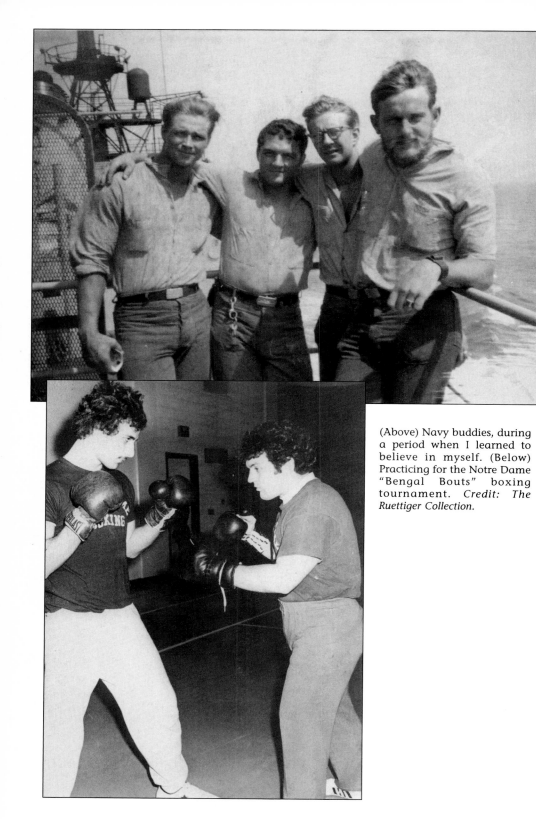

(Above) Navy buddies, during a period when I learned to believe in myself. (Below) Practicing for the Notre Dame "Bengal Bouts" boxing tournament. *Credit: The Ruettiger Collection.*

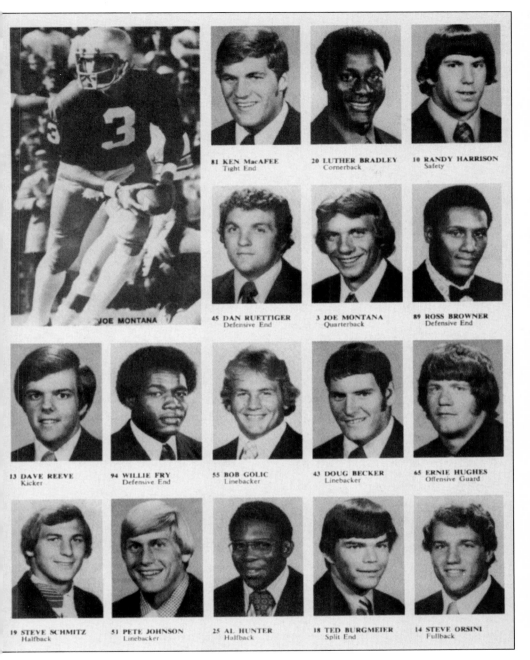

JOE MONTANA

81 KEN MacAFEE
Tight End

20 LUTHER BRADLEY
Cornerback

10 RANDY HARRISON
Safety

45 DAN RUETTIGER
Defensive End

3 JOE MONTANA
Quarterback

89 ROSS BROWNER
Defensive End

13 DAVE REEVE
Kicker

94 WILLIE FRY
Defensive End

55 BOB GOLIC
Linebacker

43 DOUG BECKER
Linebacker

65 ERNIE HUGHES
Offensive Guard

19 STEVE SCHMITZ
Halfback

51 PETE JOHNSON
Linebacker

25 AL HUNTER
Halfback

18 TED BURGMEIER
Split End

14 STEVE ORSINI
Fullback

A page from the game-day program of the 1975 Notre Dame vs. Georgia Tech game, the day my first dream came true, reprinted by Tri-Star for promotional purposes.

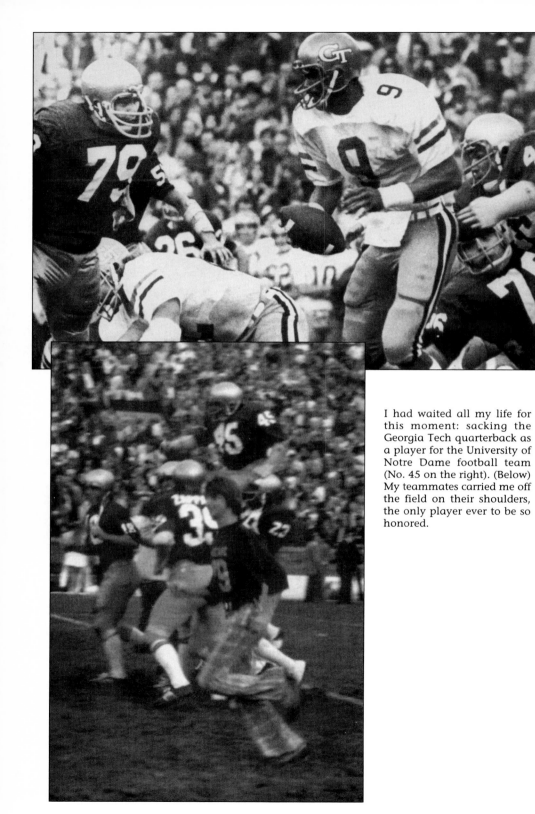

I had waited all my life for this moment: sacking the Georgia Tech quarterback as a player for the University of Notre Dame football team (No. 45 on the right). (Below) My teammates carried me off the field on their shoulders, the only player ever to be so honored.

1975 NOTRE DAME
FOOTBALL TEAM

I almost missed this one. After bitterly quitting the team for being left off the game list for the last time, I overcame my pride and returned to practice in time for the team picture (No. 45) and to find out I would dress for the game. This one decision changed my whole life.

Sean Astin as me, in an empty Notre Dame locker room, emphatically re-enacting Knute Rockne's famous speech I learned on the radio as a kid: "We're going to go inside, we're going to go outside. We're not going to quit until we cross that goalline. Today's the day we're going to lick 'em. Now let's get out there and get 'em!" *Credit: Tri-Star Pictures.*

Me and Tri-Star President Mark Platt. *Credit: Tri-Star Pictures.*

My brothers with Sean Astin the day we filmed the game sequences: Timmy, Mick, Johnny, Mark, Francis, and Bernie.

(Above) Writer and co-producer Angelo Pizzo (left) and director David Anspaugh. (Below) Producers Robert Fried (left) and Cary Woods (right). These guys believed in my dream and were the muscle behind getting it through the Hollywood roadblocks. *Credit: Tri-Star Pictures.*

ngelo Pizzo, Sean Astin, and me at the premiere of "Rudy" in my hometown, Joliet, Illinois. *Credit:*
arry W. Kane.

When

people say

dreams

don't come true,

tell them

about

RUDY

Another impossible dream realized: The making of "Rudy." (Inset) The beginning of a new drea encouraging people as a motivational speaker, particularly to salespeople and students. *Credit: T Dunkes, New Philadelphia (OH) Times Reporter.*

play I sack the quarterback. My teammates, who had done everything they could to help get me into that game, carried me off the field on their shoulders. It was the only time that has happened in the history of Notre Dame football. It was, as they used to say in the trade magazines, a boffo ending.

But in real life, I had two chances to get the quarterback. The first play, I didn't get there in time. I was too anxious and didn't execute the play. I failed.

When Georgia Tech, our opponents, lined up for the last play of the game, there were five seconds on the clock. I knew this was the last chance I would ever get. When they snapped the ball, I wasn't worried about failing. I'd done that already, and I knew why I had failed. That's how you eliminate that fear. You keep learning until you have the confidence to perform when you have to. That's why football players work so hard. The more films you watch, the more weights you lift, the more you study the playbook, the greater your confidence and the less your fear of failure. In its place is courage.

That's what I had when they snapped the ball for the last time. I put the moves I'd rehearsed in my mind on the guy over me and I got to the quarterback. It was my last chance ever and I was ready for it.

Michael Jordan failed in his first try to make his high school basketball team. Casey Stengel failed at his first attempt at managing. Mickey Mantle failed in his first shot at the major leagues. Willie Mays failed in his first months in the big leagues. Abraham Lincoln is remembered for his great debates with Steven Douglas in his first race for the U.S. Senate. What people forget is that Lincoln lost—he failed. Lincoln failed many other times. He went bankrupt once. He even thought that his Gettysburg Address, considered to be one of the greatest speeches in history, was a failure. Dr. Seuss, the greatest writer of children's books ever, failed more than a hundred times to get his first book published. Lou Holtz, one of the most successful football coaches in Notre Dame history, failed miserably in an attempt to coach in the pros.

John Starks, the all-star guard for the New York Knicks, failed in his first attempt to make the pros. Thomas Edison probably had as many inventions that failed as he had ones that succeeded. Vincent Van Gogh thought he was a total failure as a painter; he sold only one of his paintings during his life, and that to his brother.

The list goes on and on. Show me someone who's succeeded spectacularly, and I'll guarantee you that he or she has failed. President Clinton failed to win reelection after his first term as governor of Arkansas. Without that failure, he admits, he never would have become president.

Obviously, failure isn't as awful as it's made out to be. The key is that every person I've mentioned and everyone else who's come back from failure refused to dwell on it. I failed. Okay, what can I learn from it? What positives can I take from that? Forget the negatives. I know all about them and they're history.

That's how you have to look at it. We fail for a reason, and the key is not to be ashamed to have failed but to discover that reason so that the next time we won't fail—at least not for the same reason.

I'm not going to kid you. Failure isn't easy. There were times I'd be so depressed I didn't know what I was going to do. I didn't want to go on. But what they say is true. When things look their worst is when it's going to start to get better. When the situation is darkest, that's when you're closest to success.

You have to believe that. You must have faith. That's another rule:

When the situation looks hopeless, you have to reach for your faith.

My faith is in my roots and the values I learned as a child. And it's in God.

You see a lot of people—a lot of kids—who don't have any

faith. They don't believe that there's something better. They don't believe there's a God who doesn't want them to suffer and is ready to help them if only they ask. That has to be awful.

I tell kids that when I speak in schools. I tell them that faith got me where I am. When I'm filled with doubt and despair, I pray. I ask God for help, for strength. If you don't have that, it's going to be tough to deal with obstacles and challenges and failure. Because that's when you dig and dig and dig and find there's nothing there.

So you have to believe in something. I'm not saying it has to be the Catholic God I grew up with. It can be the higher power that people in twelve-step programs like Alcoholics Anonymous accept. I don't care if it's a tree. Just as long as there's something that you can turn to; something you can believe in. You've got to have that for when the situation looks the most bleak. Because if you can just get through that, the good stuff is going to be there for you.

And when you get there, all the failure and the despair are going to make it more wonderful than anything you've ever known before. It's like when you're playing baseball and the pitcher strikes you out three times and you never touch the ball. Then you get up in the last inning and hit a home run off the guy to win the game. Hitting a home run is always great. But you'll remember that one forever because of the failure that went before it. It's why baseball players love the game so well. Even the best hitters fail seven out of ten times. And the seven failures make the three successes that much better.

Just because failure is necessary doesn't mean you have to enjoy it or seek it out. And there are ways to avoid failure. One of them is this:

Don't worry about the other guy. Worry about yourself.

That's one of the reasons I failed academically in high school. Yes, I am dyslexic, but it was more than that. In high school, I competed in the classroom with the other guys.

Instead of trying to work to my potential, I was trying to beat the smart guys. When I couldn't, it just made me miserable and finally made me quit trying.

When I got to Holy Cross, Brother John took me aside and said, "Rudy, don't worry about what everybody else is doing. Worry about yourself. You've got to get the grades. What don't you understand? We're not here to flunk you. If you flunk, you'll flunk yourself."

When I stopped worrying about keeping up with or beating the other students, I could focus on my own work. And it works. It really works.

And not just in college. I don't know how many salesmen I've seen go nuts trying to beat another salesman. Why is that guy selling more cars than me? Why is that woman selling more houses? Or insurance? Or widgets? I make just as many phone calls. I wear the same shirts. I use the same deodorant. Man, I've got to beat him.

Who says you do? The only person you can compete with is yourself. If you dream big, that's competition enough.

I never told anyone else on the football team how I really viewed myself. They would have laughed at me even more. But I always thought of myself as a starter. I had to think that way to survive. It allowed me to go out there every day and get my butt kicked and come back for more. It allowed me to keep going.

Some of the other guys told me, "Rudy, get the heck out of here. You're going to get killed." But that was my choice, not theirs. It was like when the guys at the plant asked me, "How are you going to compete with those guys at Notre Dame, Rudy? They're smarter than you."

And the way I did it is I didn't think about it. I didn't compete with them. Let them get their grades. Let them start. But let me try to get my grades, and let me try to start, too. And if you get better grades or get higher on the depth chart, I won't take it personally. Because it's not personal. And if I've done my best, that's all I can ask for.

That's what life is about. It's not about winning or losing. I say that to the football teams I talk to, and I believe it. If you play the best game you can and give every drop of effort you have, then you're a winner. Don't judge everything by the scoreboard; by who scored more points or sold more cars. These people who measure success only by winning championships have it all wrong. I don't believe in national champions. I believe everybody who tries their best is a champion.

Here's another rule for you:

It's only a game.

I don't mean just football. I mean life. It's all the same. People lose a football game or they lose a big sale or they don't get the promotion and they think it's going to ruin the rest of their lives. It will if they let it. But, hey, there'll be another game, another sale, another promotion. It doesn't mean that you don't care. Not caring is a recipe for failure. What it means is that all you can do is your best. If it doesn't work, okay. Try another approach. It's like Joe Montana says, "I care, but not that much."

There's a certain sense of humor in that; a healthy perspective. Tug McGraw, a great relief pitcher in the '60s and '70s for the Mets and Phillies, had a great way of putting it. He called it "The Cosmic Ice Ball Theory."

McGraw was a closer, which meant that he was always being called into games when his team was hanging onto a slim lead in the ninth inning. It always seemed that there were men on base and some monster like Willie Stargell, the great first baseman for the Pirates, would be at the plate, waiting for McGraw to throw a pitch so he could hit it out of the park and win the game.

McGraw said that he didn't really want to throw the ball to Willie Stargell, because when it disappeared over the wall, McGraw would go from hero to villainous failure. What he really wanted to do was hold the ball until everyone got bored and went home. But he knew that sooner or later the umpire would make him throw that ball to Willie Stargell.

So McGraw would remind himself of The Cosmic Ice Ball Theory. And that is when, according to scientists, in about five billion years, the sun will burn out and the earth will be a cosmic ice ball hurtling through space. And when that happens, no one will care what he did pitching to Willie Stargell in the bottom of the ninth inning.

So he threw the ball. Usually, he got Stargell or whoever was up there out. Sometimes he didn't. Either way, in only five billion years, there wouldn't be anyone around to care.

History doesn't care. This wonderful and changing era that we live in is the greatest of all eras. That's how we tend to look at things. The media age helps reinforce that idea. Every success or failure gets magnified to mythic proportions. But five hundred years from now, we'll be lucky if we rate a paragraph in an eighth-grade history book.

People are so concerned with how the world will look at them. But in fifty years how many people will know who Joey Buttafuoco and Amy Fisher were? How many will have more than a vague idea of what Donald Trump did?

So quit worrying about what people will think if you fail. There's no shame in it. The worst thing that can happen is that you fail so spectacularly that people remember you for a long time. And when you come down to it, that's better than not being remembered at all.

The best thing that can happen is that you'll be remembered for more than Andy Warhol's fifteen minutes of fame. That's why you have to take risks in life. I'm not saying you have to go over Niagara Falls in a barrel or that you have to be the first to climb Mt. Everest naked. And I'm not saying you should take the mortgage down to Atlantic City and put it on the black at the nearest roulette wheel.

The risks you take should be calculated. They should be risks you understand, risks that make sense. You have to figure out the maximum downside you can afford, and then go for it.

Taking risks is basic to human nature. My grandparents took a huge risk when they left their homes in Europe to come to America. The pioneers took enormous risks to settle the frontier. The Founding Fathers risked their lives to establish this country and build the first modern democracy.

For all of these people, the cost of failure was greater than anything most of us will ever face. But they took the risk, and we should thank them every day for it.

In today's society, we seem to spend all of our spare time manufacturing risks. We go bungee jumping, which seems like a risk, and feels like a risk, but really isn't. We go rock climbing and mountain biking and tear through the countryside on dirt bikes and snowmobiles.

I'm not knocking any of that. It's fun to do those things. But those risks are physical. The real fun, the real risk and the thrill that goes with it, comes when you put your inner self—your convictions, beliefs, and self-image—on the line.

People try to talk us out of that kind of risk. That's really what my father was doing when he told me to forget about going to Notre Dame and stay at the plant. He didn't want to see me crash and burn and have my self-image utterly destroyed. That's what he was supposed to do. I guess the guys who made fun of me at work were supposed to do it, too.

But I don't care if I crash and burn. In fact, if I do fail, I want to fail so spectacularly that everyone will see it. If I go up in flames, I want it to be a fireball that's seen across ten states and two Canadian provinces. I don't want to lose because Willie Stargell hit a broken-bat single off me. If I'm going to go down, I want Stargell to hit it into the next area code.

That's because you can only fail spectacularly if your dreams are really big. If I had wanted to go to just any college, I could have gotten into a state school. As long as you have a high school diploma, they have to take you. And if I had wanted to play college football, I could have found someplace to do that, too. I was a decent player in high school. I could have been a starter in a Division II or III school.

But that's not what I wanted. That dream wasn't big enough. I wanted a special dream about a special place, and Notre Dame, for me, was that place. It was the same with the movie. I could have made a television movie much more easily than a major motion picture. But if I was going to get a movie made, I wanted it on the big screen. If someone wanted to put it on television, let them rent it at the video store.

You've got to look at your life the same way. If your dream is to go to college, you may as well aim for a good one. If it's to be an officer in the Navy, don't be satisfied with being a second lieutenant. Go for admiral. If you want to be president of a company, make it a big company.

Just be aware that one of the risks that goes along with those big dreams is the jealousy that is sure to follow. It's amazing how people will like you just fine as long as you're at their level, but the minute you start to realize your dream and start to achieve something better, they get jealous. Those are the people who say, "That Rudy's such a pest." Or they say, "Rudy's just a self-proclaimed hero."

I'm neither of those things. I don't think of myself as a hero. If I'm a self-proclaimed anything, it's a self-proclaimed dreamer. And I don't think it's being a pest to go back to Angelo Pizzo to give him a chance to see how his dreams coincided with mine. There's a difference between persistence and being a pest; namely, knowing when to back off and when to push. That's the secret to getting things done.

But people get jealous mainly because they didn't have the courage themselves to achieve their dreams. Instead of going after what they wanted, instead of being the person they believed themselves to be, they sat around and talked about the raw deal they got. They were always overlooked. They never got the job they wanted. They got a bad deal on their house.

What I say if you didn't get that job is, so what? It's a game and failure is built into it. Even if you didn't get it, you should have learned something. Go out and get another job. Then come back when you've got some experience and get the job you really want. I look at everything that way. If you fail once, don't worry. You'll get it eventually. You just have to keep after it.

When you do get there, someone will be jealous. If you're like me, you'll be called an overachiever, as if that somehow explains what happened. Somehow, it comes out sounding like something's wrong with you.

I don't think of myself as an overachiever. After all, I didn't achieve more than I set out to do. I didn't try to do more than was possible. That's what overachieving is. And this is another lesson:

There's no such thing as an overachiever.

What people really mean when they call you an overachiever is that they are underachievers. It's what athletes are really saying when they talk about going out in that big game and giving 110 percent. You can't give 110 percent because you only have 100 percent. That's it. After that, there isn't any more.

Reggie Jackson used to say that giving 110 percent was nonsense. Most people, most of the time, are lucky to get up to 50 percent. The key, Reggie liked to say, is giving as much as you need to get the job done. Some days that might be 50 percent. Other days it might be 80 percent. And, once in a while, you may be able to get all the way to the bottom of the well and, if only for one grand moment, give everything that's there. Reggie did it in the 1977 World Series when he hit three home runs on three straight pitches. Other times he came close. He's in baseball's hall of fame now, and he got there not by giving 110 percent, but by giving everything he could when it mattered the most.

But even Reggie was an underachiever. He admitted that he couldn't crank himself up every day for every at-bat. Big moments—and the huge risk of failure that go with them—

were what he lived on.

The truth is, we're almost all underachievers. For a long time after I graduated from Notre Dame, I was an underachiever because I wasn't doing everything I could. I wasn't getting everything I could out of what I had.

There's a lot more all of us can do if we will only overcome our fear of failure and take the risk of finding out just how much we have inside us.

We do ourselves a tremendous disservice when we look at someone who has been successful without great resources and call him an overachiever. Because if we do that, we have to call Michael Jordan an overachiever, too. That sounds silly. After all, he has great talent. But so do a lot of other players who never reach the top of their sports. The difference is that Jordan got as much out of his talent as he could. Others have had the same opportunities, but didn't seize it. Jordon did. If I overachieved, so did Michael Jordan.

Otherwise, what we're saying is that some of us achieve too much. And how is that possible? If you overfill a suitcase, it doesn't close. If you overfill your gas tank, it overflows. If you overact in a screen test, you don't get the role.

What we're trying to say when we call someone an overachiever is that he or she achieved too much. And that's not possible. All we can ever achieve is what we're capable of. It's just that most of us have no idea just how much we can really do.

And we never will know if we look at failure as the enemy to be avoided at all costs. It is the fear of failure more than anything that keeps us from trying our hardest. It is far easier to give a partial effort and fail. Then we have an excuse. But if we give a total effort and fail, it's much harder to deal with.

But we don't really know what a total effort is. I thought I'd done everything I could in my first year at Holy Cross. Notre Dame told me I hadn't; that I'd failed to do enough to get in. It hurt almost more than I could bear. But I learned from that. I went back for another year. I found there was more to give and more to risk.

And as long as there's one phone call you haven't made, one bramble-filled path you haven't tried to follow, you haven't totally failed, because there's still more effort to give. You haven't gotten to 100 percent yet.

And if you do get to that point, where you can't think of anything else you can do, ask yourself honestly: Have I given everything I have? If the answer is yes, there's no shame. You've learned a lot, and you've had an adventure few people ever have. When you dream again—and you must dream again—you'll be better prepared to reach your new dream.

Remember, the shame isn't in failing, it's in not trying. And remember, too, that life isn't meant to be happy all the time. Unless you have sorrow, you can never truly experience joy. And the harder the struggle, the greater the reward at journey's end. Finally, you can not possibly appreciate the true meaning of victory unlesss you have also met defeat.

RUDY'S RULE #6

Get the Dollar Signs Out of Your Eyes

6

Before I made my movie, I had ten jobs and got fired from five of them. The others I quit.

One reason I failed was because I wasn't doing what I really wanted to do. But another reason was because my expectations were totally wrong. Too many times, I got into a business because I thought I was going to make a lot of money.

There's nothing wrong with making money. It's only wrong when that's your primary objective. Ultimately you'll fail, because money isn't what it's about. Doing what you truly want to do is.

When I made my movie, I can't tell you how many people came up to me and asked me how much money I made on it. That's how we're raised to think in this country. How much did you make? Not, What does it mean to you? Or, Gee, but that's an inspiring movie! Or even, How did you do it?

No, it's just, How much did you make, Rudy? And, I guess you're rich now, Rudy.

If you really have to know, I didn't end up with much at all. It cost me almost everything I made for the movie rights to pay off all the people I had dealt with along the way who thought they owned a piece of the movie. The guy who wrote a script and walked off with my credit cards wound up with $70,000—a lot more than I did. Everybody said, "Rudy, you're nuts paying this guy any more money!" But I didn't care about the money. It didn't matter to me if I made a nickel or a million bucks. The message was what was important to me. That's why I wanted to make the movie; to let other people know they could dream, too. And if I had to pay a guy $70,000 right now rather than hold the whole project up for who knows how long while I went to court, I was paying the money.

But that's how we keep score—by how much you have in the bank, what kind of car you drive, how big your house is, what fancy prep school your kids go to, what the label is inside your suits.

I was just as susceptible to that as anyone. When I first went out into the world to make a living, I thought that the object was to have the nice, imported car like the boss had. I thought I was supposed to run out and buy that big house in the suburbs. That's being confused. It's not keeping things simple.

And it's the wrong score. It's like deciding who won a football game not by who has more points, but by who has fancier uniforms. Appearances and money become so important, we forget that the real purpose of life is to make the world a better place for our children. The way you do that is by helping people, not by taking as much money as you can from them.

I quit one insurance job because of that. They taught us how to sell people policies they didn't need, and how to add things on to the policy to get a bigger commission. They taught us deception instead of honesty.

That just ruins it for everyone, yourself included. Insurance is important. Selling it is an honorable job. But people like the ones I worked for give it a bad name. They make insurance salesmen the punch line in a bad joke. All because they don't have their values straight. They'll go to church and demand that the government do something about crime, and then bright and early Monday morning they're selling some poor schmuck something he doesn't need. They're stealing, and they call it making a living. And it's easy to get caught up in it—if the way you keep score is by how much you make.

Chasing that almighty dollar totally messes up your dreams. Go into a school to talk about your job, and before long kids will be asking you how much money you make. That's how they make their career decisions. But how can you chase a dream if the only thing you're thinking of is how much money you'll make? You can't.

When I talk to groups of people in the real estate industry, I tell them straight out that if they got into the business so they could make a lot of money, they won't last a year. The reason for that is that you don't just walk into a real estate job and start putting up big balances in your checking account. It takes a long time to be successful in that business. When the people who get into it for the money realize that they're not raking it in like they thought, they quit. They quit because they never really enjoyed it in the first place.

It's the difference between a career and a job. When I was at that power plant, I had a job. All the other things I did to make a living were jobs, too. But now, finally, I have a career. I'm a motivational speaker. I always wanted to do that; to help people get out of the ruts they're in. I think I'm good at it, and I love doing it. And when you love what you do, you're just amazed and delighted that they pay you for having so much fun.

But there's another job I want to do, too. This is one of those dreams that people laugh at, because it's so simple. But here it is: I want to cut the grass in Notre Dame Stadium. That's it. I don't even care if they pay me. I just want to have something to do with the place I love. I'll wash football uniforms, paint the lines, do anything, just to be involved. I haven't gotten that job yet because no one believes that after all I've done I don't have some hidden agenda. They think I want to take over the place or something. Or they don't think the job pays enough for me. Or something. I don't know. I just want to do it because it would be fun, like a hobby. Someday I will, too.

I realize that we all have to make a living, but when you look at jobs you might take and careers you might follow, ask yourself why you want to do it. Assume you're not going to get paid at all and ask yourself if it would still be fun.

That means cut out all the things that you think might go with it. Don't look at the problems or the material rewards. That's not why we dream; at least it's not why we should dream. It's not about getting rich or having an enormous house and a Mercedes in the drive. It's about doing what you want to do, being what you want to be.

I have a rule I try to follow in making that kind of decision. It's this:

Don't do what you think you might want to do. Do what you *know* you want to do.

As soon as you say, "I think I want to do this," you're in trouble. When you find yourself in that position, and it's going to happen, you have to start asking yourself some questions. Write them down and write out the answers and see what you come up with. Look at the reasons why it's the right decision and the reasons it's the wrong one.

Like when I decided I wanted to play football at Notre Dame. The wrong reason would have been because I thought I was going to be a pro and make a lot of money. That wasn't going to happen. It was unrealistic. The right reasons were, first, because that had always been my dream. Second, I enjoyed the camaraderie of being part of a team. Third, I could see myself doing it. Fourth, it filled my need for risk and adventure and a physical challenge.

Money wasn't part of it beyond the fact that if I made the team, I'd be able to eat. But if that had been my only reason for going out, I probably wouldn't have made it. Money just isn't that important.

Yet, we make it out to be everything. One of our favorite pastimes is complaining about how much money professional athletes make. And it's true, they make a ton of money. But it's also true that most professional golfers, for instance, would still be playing golf even if it didn't pay a penny. Baseball players would still be playing ball. It might be in the local church league, or on a tavern team or the company team, but they'd be playing as often as they could, just like so many of us did and do. They're blessed because it just worked out that they can get a lot of money for playing a game they love. But for most of them, first came the love of the game. The money is incidental.

Now, say you are thinking about real estate as a career. Maybe you already have your license and you're struggling, wondering when you're going to be able to buy that BMW and move into that big house with the hot tub. It's probably not happening the way you thought it would and you're thinking of quitting.

The first thing you do is look at why you're in it. Do you like meeting all different kinds of people? Do you love dealing in certain kinds of real estate—commercial, old houses, starter houses, luxury houses? Do you like being your own boss and setting your own hours? These are all good reasons to be in real estate.

You have to love the product you sell. And don't kid yourself, we're all salesmen. Chuck Daly, the basketball coach who led the Dream Team in the 1992 Olympics and won two world championships with the Detroit Pistons, preaches that. He has to sell his system and his strategies to his players every day. A newspaper reporter has to sell her story ideas to the editor. An animal trainer has to sell his authority to his animals. An actor has to sell his performance to the audience. A policeman has to sell his control and confidence to everyone he meets. The president has to sell his programs. We might not look at it as selling, but it's part of every job.

And if you love your product and believe in it, the money

will come to you. If you don't, you'll soon be looking for another job.

So you have to realize that any career is a long-term commitment. It's like a marriage, and if you're in it for the love of it, it gets better as the years go by. All sales jobs work the same way.

When you take the dollar signs out of your eyes, you stop trying to make the big sale every day. You don't try to force people into something they can't afford and isn't right for them, whether it's a car, a house, or an insurance policy. You start looking at clients as people you can help. You take an interest in their needs and take the time to qualify them so that when you show them your product, you can match them to what they want.

The size of the commission isn't important if you have enough of them. The way you get them is to treat your job with the respect a career deserves. Do all the little things. Listen to your customers. People will remember you if you treat them right. They'll send their friends to you to buy or to list their homes. If you're in real estate, after years of work, you'll find that you can live wonderfully just on listings. Other salesmen are doing the work, and you're sharing in the rewards. And you'll be making that money because you put people first and let the rest come to you.

It's like getting *Rudy* made. I helped David and Angelo fulfill their dreams and they helped me fulfill mine. Notre Dame let me film on campus because *Rudy* fulfilled their dream to portray the university as a place where ordinary people do extraordinary things.

You're doing the same thing when you're selling a house or a car. People have dreams about where they want to live and what they want to drive. You're there to help them get that. So you don't show them what's good for you. You show them what's right for them. That's another rule I try to live by:

Dreams don't happen unless you help other people.

Oh, you'll meet people or read about people who set out to be rich and famous and succeeded. They'd say I'm nuts. They did it without worrying about others. You can, too.

And you can, if that's what you want. But you'll hurt a lot of people along the way, and sooner or later that comes back to you. You'll know it deep inside and you'll be empty. It's just not worth it. And it's not necessary, either.

I had no intention of becoming famous by making *Rudy*. Yet, one day soon after the movie came out, I was giving a speech in San Diego when I got a call from the White House. President and Mrs. Clinton wanted me to come to dinner and a screening of the movie. When I was a kid, getting invited to the White House was something you didn't even dare to dream about. And here I was, a guy from Joliet, being invited to have dinner with the president. Wow!

The first thing I did was call my father: "Hey, Dad. You'll never believe where I'm going! To the White House!"

It's so much better when you're not expecting it. You fly into Washington, D.C., and tell the cab driver at the airport, "Take me to the White House." When I got there, they put me in a room to wait, and then the doors opened and Hillary Clinton walked in, all excited to meet me! She took me up to this little theater they have and she introduced me to the president. And he put his arm around my shoulder like I was his old buddy and introduced me to all these people I read about in the newspapers and see on television. Chelsea was there with a friend. John Glenn was there. They were acting like it was a big deal to meet me.

And when the movie was over, everyone applauded. Hillary Clinton stood up and said, "Every child in America should see this movie."

I was thrilled and I was proud. I chased the dream of my movie for a lot of years and through a lot of agony because I thought it had a message that people needed to hear. And that made me feel that my dream had really come true.

Imagine if I had quit because it was costing me all my money. That never would have happened. I never would have gotten letters from school kids all across the country telling me how they'd been inspired by my story. A lot of people who got new hope would still be locked in despair.

But it happened, and that's what comes of big dreams. It's what happens when you forget about money.

When I went to Hollywood to finally sign with Tri-Star to make *Rudy*, I didn't have what anyone would call a real job. I had been the finance and insurance manager at an auto dealership. At the start of the year, the owner of the dealership asked me what my goals were for the coming year. I told him I wanted to help him sell a lot of cars and I wanted to get my movie made.

The owner looked at me and said that my dream didn't fit in with his. If I was still going to be running around chasing *Rudy*, it would be taking me away from what he wanted to do, and he didn't want that. I wouldn't give up on my dream, so I lost the job.

I went back to South Bend, where I live, and got a job as the maintenance man at my condominium project. I shoveled the snow in the winter and cut the grass in the summer. That was my job. When the call came to go to Hollywood to sign, I had $56 in my checking account. That was my entire fortune.

But I wasn't worried, because I knew I could always make more money. But I couldn't miss a chance at a dream. Nobody can.

RUDY'S RULE #7

Quit Making Excuses

How many times have you heard this line: "I really should be doing such-and-so, but I don't feel like it today?" Go ahead, admit it. You've probably said it yourself.

Maybe you meant to do something, but you decided you couldn't get up early enough to do it. Or you meant to send that résumé out, but you didn't have a stamp and the post office was closed. Or you were going to tackle a big job, but decided that something else that you hadn't thought about for months simply had to be done first.

Well, the reality is that if you want to catch up to your dreams, you have to do certain things. You know it, I know it. We all know it, and still we find ways to avoid taking the steps we know are necessary.

What we're really talking about here is commitment. Until you make a commitment to your dream, it's not a dream at all. It's just another fantasy. And fantasies don't come true, because they're not real; we're not committed to them. But when we make that commitment, they become dreams. And dreams are very real.

I've talked about how you have to decide who you really are, and what you want to do. That's where the commitment comes in.

So what is commitment? It's eliminating excuses.

That's how I got to Notre Dame. I eliminated excuses. Making the football team was the same. And believe me, I had excuses galore.

Like most people who don't pursue their dreams, at first, I didn't think I was making excuses. I thought there were good reasons for not going to Notre Dame. I didn't have the grades or the S.A.T. scores. I needed to work. Guys like me didn't go to Notre Dame. And the longer I stayed in Joliet, the more I could say I was too old.

To reasonable people—my teachers, my parents—this all made sense. But, as I found, being reasonable isn't always all it's cracked up to be. After all, what is reasonable, and what is unreasonable? Is it reasonable to say that two preteen girls couldn't fly an ultralight airplane across the United States? You'd have to say yes. But not long ago, two girls did just that.

From the beginning of the modern Olympics in 1896, it was considered unreasonable—impossible, really—for women to run a marathon. Until a couple of decades ago, it wasn't even allowed. Women weren't strong enough to run so far. They didn't have the stamina. They could get hurt or die. Most people thought that was reasonable.

But today, women run marathons and they run them fast. Women play hockey and basketball and baseball and soccer. They do a lot of things that reasonable people said they couldn't do.

The list goes on and on of what we once thought unreasonable. African-Americans couldn't play major-league baseball. A man who was only five-foot-eight couldn't play in the National Basketball Association, and one who was six-foot-eight couldn't play point guard. But Jackie Robinson proved otherwise in baseball, Muggsy Bogues and Spudd Webb proved that short men could play with the giants, and Magic Johnson changed forever the way we look at point guards.

As it turned out, the reasonable people were only making

excuses. The pioneers who blazed new trails recognized that. They decided what they wanted to do, not what others wanted, and they eliminated all those excuses.

When I finally committed myself to going to Notre Dame and then to making the football team, that's what I did. I found out that not having the grades was an excuse. There was a way to get them at Holy Cross. My lack of size and speed in football was an excuse, too. Desire and hard work counted more.

If I had dwelled on how hard it would be to play football, or how difficult it would be to get into Notre Dame, I never would have done it. I'd still be working in that power plant. So once I made the commitment, I didn't think of any of those things. I just did it.

Sometimes, it's best not to know too much. Big businesses won't do anything without first spending huge amounts of money on market research. If the research tells them they have a good idea, they go ahead. If it says the idea isn't any good, they don't. So why do so many allegedly good ideas not work out? And how do regular folks make dreams come true without conducting a shred of research?

Colonel Sanders didn't commission a big study to find out if people would eat his chicken. He knew it was good and that was enough for him. Famous Amos and Mrs. Fields didn't look at the cookie market and say, "Oh, there are too many chocolate chip cookies out there already. No one will ever buy mine." They knew they had a good product and they went ahead and started, and neither one of them really knew how they were going to make it happen. They just refused to accept excuses.

It was the same with my movie. There were a million reasons—excuses—not to keep after that dream. I decided at the beginning I wasn't going to think about them. It was the only way to get it done. Knowing too much would have stopped me before I started.

The 1993 University of Wisconsin football team was the same way. They had tons of excuses not to excel. They weren't blue-chip recruits out of high school. Wisconsin never won football games before, so why should they? The other teams were bigger, faster, better.

What made the Badgers win was commitment. Excuses weren't going to cut it any more. They were going to do the work, put out the supreme effort, stand by their teammates. They were going to be winners.

A big part of Wisconsin's success came from that concept of teamwork. We like to talk about that a lot in this country. Companies are always talking about teamwork. We teach our kids about it. But are we really committed to it?

Too often, we say we are, but we aren't. We let ourselves be stopped by jealousy. It's easy to see on a sports team. One player gets jealous of another who is getting more playing time. When it comes time for the jealous player to go in, he's too consumed by his emotions to do the job he's supposed to do. Maybe he tries to do everything himself to show that other kid who's better.

That's a recipe for failure, both team and individual. It's the same way in business. You can't be jealous of Mary because she sold more houses than you did. You can't be jealous of Joe because he has a better car or a bigger house. It becomes an excuse: Why bother when Mary or Joe is going to get all the good jobs?

Jealousy stops you from doing things; it stops you from achieving your dreams. Instead of worrying about the other person getting ahead of you, help that person achieve his or her own goals. Be happy for that person. If you help others get to the next level, you'll be surprised to find that they'll take you along with them.

Let me give you another rule:

To eliminate excuses, you have to accept responsibility.

It's all part of making a commitment. And it's a big part of getting to where you want to go, because dreams carry with them a lot of responsibility.

Maybe taking the next step in your business means coming in early for extra meetings. Well, if you're going to do that, you can't stay up until three in the morning firing down shots and beers with the boys. That's not being responsible. If you want your marriage to work, it's the same thing.

Or maybe your dream is to be sales manager in your office. If so, you have to realize that when you get there, you will have many more responsibilities. When you're a manager, you can't worry just about yourself. The people working under you have families. The company has goals. All these things become your business. You can't make excuses.

Here's another excuse: "I can't do that because I don't know how."

It's like I used to think when I first thought I wanted to be the president of the insurance company and then decided I didn't know how to do it. What I didn't realize then is that if I wanted to be president, then I had a responsibility to learn everything there was to know about that job. Saying I couldn't learn it was an excuse.

When I was in real estate, I saw deals fall through in the closing room because the agent was caught unprepared. Something came up, and he didn't know the answer. And afterwards, he complained that the other guys purposely tried to catch him off guard. Yeah, that was it. He got screwed.

Maybe the other guy was trying to screw him, but it's still an excuse. The agent's responsibility was to be prepared for any contingency. Any time you're getting ready to close any deal, you can't go in without knowing everything that can come up. This is not a time when the less you know the better.

If you're selling cars, you have to know everything there is to know about those cars. You have to know why your car is right for the person buying it. If they ask you why thirty-two valves are better than sixteen valves, you better know the answer.

And when you make the sale, your responsibility isn't

finished. That customer just invested a lot of money in your product, so you better be ready to help when the customer calls you asking about different things that maybe aren't working right. You have to know how the warranty and service agreements work. You can't just shove that customer off on someone else. Because if you don't show that you care— and it is your responsibility to care—you'll never see that customer again. Not only that, but the customer will tell his or her friends to stay away from your dealership. Your lack of knowledge or consideration or your excuse that you just didn't have the time to take care of it can wind up costing everyone who works there a lot of money.

So even though a lot of knowledge isn't important to get started in something, it is very important as you continue toward your goal. I didn't have to know everything it was going to take to get into Notre Dame right away, but once I started on the road to my dream, I had to learn. Just getting into Holy Cross wasn't going to get me into Notre Dame. I had to have knowledge to do that.

Knowing what I had to know eliminated another excuse: I couldn't understand what the professors were talking about. Just about everyone has had that experience. Someone's trying to teach you something, but you just don't get it; it doesn't register. That becomes an excuse.

When I didn't think I could get good grades, I used that excuse all the time. But when I had to get good grades, I realized that you're allowed to ask the professor to explain it again. At Notre Dame, and at Holy Cross, the students helped one another as well.

You learn there's no such thing as a stupid question. You ask questions so that you can learn. And when I got in an atmosphere in which people wanted me to succeed, they didn't mind my asking. They didn't think of me as being stupid. They wanted to help.

So if we should always ask questions when we don't understand something, we also have a responsibility to help others when they ask us questions. Don't be that person who is asked a question by the new worker and says, "Who do I look like, Alex Trebeck? Go find out yourself." Be the person who helps that new worker learn and grow, and somewhere along the line, he'll help you.

It was the same with the football team. Initially, desire got me the chance, but to actually pull on those gold pants, dress in the regular locker room, run through that tunnel, get into a game, and sack the quarterback, I needed a lot of knowledge.

Not all of my teammates shared my desire. Some of them told me to quit being such a rah-rah jerk. Ease up, they said. Give me a break, they said.

I didn't worry about those guys. My goal wasn't to please them. If it had been, it would have been a great excuse not to reach my potential: "Aw, heck, I didn't want the guys to be mad at me."

My friends on the team were the players who appreciated my effort and desire. They were the ones who helped me, who answered my questions, who helped me on my technique. Together, we all got better.

When I finally got into that football game, no one expected me to actually do anything. I was last string. The only reason I got to play at all was because my teammates stood up for me. Just getting on the field would have been enough for everyone—except me.

I spent two hard and long and painful years preparing for those few seconds. I had studied my position, learned the techniques. All during the game, I didn't stand around on the sidelines waving to my dad or looking at the pretty women in the stands. I studied our starting defensive end and what he was doing to beat the other kid. If I got in, I was going to play over the same tackle, and I wanted to know how to handle him.

If I hadn't done all that, I never would have made the tackle. I wouldn't have been carried off the field. I wouldn't have made a movie. I wouldn't be giving motivational speeches and writing books.

At the time, no one would have blamed me if I didn't get the job done. I had tons of excuses. If I had gone in and had just been happy to get in my three plays, no one would have said a word. They'd have said, "Way to go, Rudy," and slapped me on the back, and that would have been the end of it.

But I didn't accept that there would be any excuses. I eliminated the excuses; swept them from my mind. And look what that's done for me.

The responsibility to eliminate excuses doesn't stop with yourself. If you're a member of a team—and almost all of us are in one way or another—you've got to help your teammates eliminate their excuses, too.

When I was putting the movie *Rudy* together, I had to do a lot of that. Angelo Pizzo didn't like Notre Dame and wasn't going to do another Indiana sports movie. He looked at that as a reason not to help me. I saw it as an excuse that was keeping him from his dream of making another feature film.

So I had to eliminate those excuses. The farther along we went, the more of them we ran into. It was one thing to give him my story and get a script. But I had to get him believing that he could do it. I had to motivate him.

I had to do the same with the Notre Dame administration. They had a terrific excuse not to allow us to film on campus. It hadn't been done in fifty years. I had to show them that there was a good reason to allow us to make the movie.

The movie could have fallen apart at any time. We had a very limited shooting schedule, and all kinds of questions kept coming up. What if we can't get people to portray the football players? How were we going to shoot an entire game sequence during six minutes of one halftime of one Notre Dame game? How was I going to clear all the claims that had been made on the rights to the movie?

That was my responsibility as story consultant on the movie. I was the official excuse eliminator. Don't worry, we'll get the players. Don't worry, we'll get the footage shot. Don't worry, I'll pay off all those guys and get the rights.

I talked about how much money it cost me to clear everything up so that the movie could be released. And that's another rule:

Money is not an excuse.

When people say they'd like to go after their dreams but they just can't afford to, what they're really saying is, "I don't want to sacrifice." And that's an excuse. Make this a rule as well:

Nothing worth having comes without sacrifice.

When I was trying to get the movie together, I had to spend a lot of money that I didn't have. But sooner or later, I had to come up with it. Because I was committed to the movie, I did. It meant working two jobs. I had my day job and then at night I went into the cleaning business. I had employees, but sometimes they didn't show up, and I had to go to office buildings and businesses and wash floors and clean toilets. It wasn't a lot of fun and I didn't get much sleep, but I was willing to do that because that's what it was going to take. And I did the job the very best I possibly could.

I finally decided that to get the movie made, it would be best for me to be living in South Bend. But at the time, I didn't have enough money to get a place to live. Right there is another excuse—a reason—to quit. But I did some research and found out that I could work out a deal to buy a condo without having a down payment.

When I got out of college, I had thought that having a swell house and a neat car were the objects of life. Once I started pursuing my dream of a movie in earnest, I learned they weren't important at all. Yes, I had to have a roof over my head and I had to have transportation, but I didn't need thirty-five hundred square feet on a hill overlooking the country club and I didn't need a BMW.

There's a big difference between what you want and what you need. You want a $50 restaurant steak, but you need a bowl of corn flakes. You want a Corvette, but what you really need is transportation. Committing myself to a dream showed me that.

When I lost my job at an auto dealership, what was I going to do? Well, there was the job opening for maintenance man at my condo complex. It would pay the mortgage and keep food on the table, and that's all I needed right then. I didn't care if all the guys in town who knew me and knew about my movie dream drove by, saw me cutting the grass, and yelled, "Hey, Rudy! How's the movie going?" Listening to those sorts had kept me in that power plant. They weren't going to keep me from another dream.

And it all paid off. When I go to speak today, I wear a $2,000 suit. I'm no better a person wearing that suit than I was when I got my suits for $49 off the rack at Robert Hall's. The only reason I have that suit is because I can afford it. If I couldn't afford it, I wouldn't have it. I'm not going to get tied up in debt buying things I can't afford, because that keeps you from going after dreams.

But when I go in front of a group, I want the best suit, the best tie, the best shirt, the best shoes I can afford so that the people I'm speaking to can see the best Rudy. I don't want them to miss my message because they're busy looking at how lousy my suit fits or how wrinkled my shirt is or how my tie doesn't match anything. I don't want to give them an excuse not to listen. And if they see that I'm successful enough to dress that nicely, they'll realize that they can get there, too.

But you don't have to start out with the best. If you think that, all you've done is given yourself an excuse not to have anything. All you need to start is a dream and commitment to it. Anything else is an excuse, and dreamers don't make excuses.

RUDY'S RULE #8

Dreams Don't Have Time Limits, But Timing Is Everything

8

Some would say that six years was my magic number. It took that long to get into Notre Dame, and it took that long to get *Rudy* made.

But there was nothing magic about six years. That's just how long it took. It could have happened sooner. It could have taken even more time. It didn't really matter. I was going to see those dreams come true no matter how long it took. I might have had to do other things along the way, but it was going to happen.

Imagine if I had told myself that I had to get into Notre Dame within five years? Or I had to get *Rudy* done in three years? It never would have happened.

Dreams are real. Time limits are artificial. Because no time is the right time and no time is the wrong time. Not for being the person you really want to be.

The only time that counts is right now.

That's it. Right now. What are you doing now to get to your dream?

That answer's easy. You're reading a motivational book. And that's a good thing to do. I read at least one a month. I listen to motivational tapes in the car. I've always done that, and I think everyone needs that constant reinforcement to keep going.

That's what it's all about. You have to maintain that enthusiasm that comes from doing what you enjoy. Sometimes, negative things happen along the way and we get discouraged. We forget that we're doing what we want to do; what we love doing. Or we start to be tempted by all the excuses that can stop us in our tracks. We forget that there is no time limit, and so the wait can seem to drag on forever.

And that's why right now is so important. If you dwell on how far you have to go, you'll never get there. So every day there has to be a right now; you have to have those little goals that get you closer to the big goal. These are the things you put time limits on. Like, "I will file my taxes today." Or if your goal is to refinish your kitchen, "I will put the new electrical boxes in by Friday." Or if you're trying to get that entry-level job in the field you want to be in, "I will send out five résumés today and I will follow up with phone calls by next Monday."

Having those little goals and meeting them makes you feel good. It fuels that enthusiasm. Other things that make you feel better about yourself are being well-groomed, making sure your clothes are neat and pressed, keeping your car clean. Again, those are things you can do right now.

The big goal—the dream—is always out there. Knowing that you're on the way to it is what counts. But while you're on that road, you can't forget about the present; about right now.

Say you want to be company president, but you're just out of school and the job you got was in the mail-room. You can't sit around fantasizing about what you'll do when you become president and blow off the mail-room job because it's not worthy of your great talents. No, you want to put everything you have into that job. You want to be the best darned mail room employee that company's ever had. You want to be just like the kid who washed the cars in the lot while he dreamed about becoming a salesman.

Now, instead of being a chore, that entry-level job becomes part of your training. And you use the time you have in that job to prepare for the next step and to understand how the department works and what kind of people work in it.

Smile. That's something else that will get you places. People like happy people. They like enthusiastic people. They like people who enjoy what they're doing. It makes them feel better not only about you, but about themselves.

Scientists have studied the act of smiling. They have discovered that even if you feel miserable, if you can summon up a genuine smile or a real laugh, you will feel better. Smiling releases chemicals in the brain that elevate your mood. So start the day with the funny papers or watch a Bugs Bunny cartoon, or the Comedy Channel if that's what it takes. But whatever you do, when you walk into that office, come in smiling. Remember this:

A positive attitude is the most important thing you can give yourself, and you have that choice every day.

At first, you might have to remind yourself to do that, because you might have fallen into the rut of whining and complaining because that's what everyone else does. But after a while, you'll find it's natural. And you'll find that the old cliché is true—time really does fly when you're having fun.

If you get out of bed and the first thing you think about is all the problems you're going to have that day, as sure as the sun rises in the east, you're going to have problems. So instead you get out of bed and say, "Hey, that miserable so-and-so is coming in first thing in the morning, and I'm going to get him. I know how to handle him. I know how to make him see I'm there to help." That means you've done your homework, you've worked out a plan, and you've come in smiling no matter how much your stomach is churning.

You'll be amazed how well that meeting can go. Because I don't care how miserable the other person is, he or she wants to get things done, too. If you can make it easier on them instead of fighting them, they'll appreciate that.

You'll be developing good habits. You'll find you really do enjoy coming into work. You'll find yourself thinking positively instead of negatively.

And make it a goal each day to learn something new about the business. That should be easy. I don't care what you're doing, there's always more you can learn about it. Go in a lawyer's office and what do you see? Shelves and shelves of law books. No lawyer knows all the law, and that's why they have the books. They know how to find it, and every day they find something new. Every day, a good lawyer gets better because he or she is always digging into those books.

You should be the same way. Build a library of books that pertain to your own career. No one knows everything about a business. What's important is knowing how to get to the knowledge you need. Great editors and writers can't live without their dictionary, thesaurus, and style book. Great public speakers read the speeches of other great speakers. Every mechanic worth his ratchet wrench has shelves of guides to every car he may have to work on.

The reason you have to keep learning and asking questions is because there is no time limit on dreams. You never know when the opportunity you've been waiting for and working for is going to arrive. And when it does, you don't want to hear yourself saying, "Maybe it's not time for me to do that yet. Maybe I'm not ready for it."

Fear of failure and maybe fear of success is at work there. But if you've been using your time, you shouldn't have those fears. Knowledge gives you confidence, so you should always be gathering knowledge, honing your skills. You should be ready, because you have to be ready.

And you will be ready if you've set those little goals and used your time well instead of frittering it away. That's called setting priorities. I can't tell you how important that is.

Prioritize everything.

What's the most important thing you have to do today? That's priority number one. What's next? And after that? Write them down and check them off as you get them done. But make sure you get them done. Because when you start prioritizing your responsibilities, things start happening. Your life starts to fall into place. You start to build up momentum, which increases your enthusiasm, which makes you eager to get up in the morning and keep it going.

Sometimes, you have to change your priorities. When I first started at Holy Cross, I dove into my books, I wrote down everything the professors said in class. I thought I was making super use of my time. And then we had our first quizzes and I flunked them all.

Well, that was my dream right there. I could have said, Ohmygosh, I'm finished. But I don't think that way. I just had to learn how to learn. With my dyslexia, I had the devil's own time with multiple choice tests. For a lot of people, those are the easiest tests. But for me they were sheer hell. So I had to make it a new top priority to learn how to take them. I talked to my professors and they showed me how to do it. My note taking obviously wasn't working, either, and again I made it a priority to find out how to take notes.

I had to do that right then because I only had a semester to get the grades I needed to stay for another semester and then to get into Notre Dame. So I would have been pretty stupid—even more stupid than the guys at the plant thought I was—to waste time running down to a bar and feeling sorry for myself. I had to do it, so I did.

That's being ready when the opportunity comes. It doesn't mean you're going to know absolutely everything. It just means you're not going to say, "No, thank you," just because you might run into some stumbling blocks along the road.

In a way, I was lucky in that I wasn't very smart in a conventional sense. Unlike a kid who gets straight A's and is the captain of the football team, I had to work and scrap for everything. And I wasn't used to getting instant results—especially in the classroom. So the idea that it was going to take a lot of hard work and a lot of time to achieve my dreams wasn't that daunting to me. Heck, I knew it was going to take me more time and effort than it did the other guy. When I decided that was what I wanted to do, I was ready to give that kind of effort.

People with more natural ability sometimes find it more difficult to deal with the idea that achieving a dream could take a long time and a lot of work. They're not used to having to scrap and struggle when they're young, and when they get older and the competition stiffens, sometimes they don't know how to compete.

The world of sports is full of players who were great as kids but who get to a certain level and then stop developing. They've finally run into people as talented as they are, and what they did on instinct when they were young isn't good enough anymore. You know who they are. They come to the pros as high draft picks and then they falter. And everyone asks, what's wrong with that guy? Why doesn't he want to work?

The answer is that he's so accustomed to instant gratification, he's unable to cope with anything else.

Probably the best thing that ever happened to Michael Jordan was not making his high school basketball team the first time he tried out. It gave him the work ethic he needed to take his natural ability to a plane that was just better than anyone else.

The opposite of the great natural talent is the kid of whom nothing is expected who somehow hits the big time and sets the world on fire. Don Mattingly was almost an afterthought in the major league draft, but he was, for a time, the best player in baseball because he had the best work ethic in baseball. Wade Boggs wasn't highly regarded at first. No one thought much of Johnny Unitas before he made the big time. Mike Piazza, the Dodger catcher who was 1993 National League Rookie of the Year, was drafted only as a favor to Dodger manager Tommy Lasorda, who knew and liked the young player. But no one in the Dodger organization thought he'd ever amount to anything.

What these stars had in common is that they had a dream—to get to the major leagues—and they didn't know when it was going to happen. Boggs, for one, who hit a ton in the minor leagues but took several years to make the big team, was upset when he'd get assigned to another year in Pawtucket. I didn't feel so well myself when I didn't get to Notre Dame after one year at Holy Cross. But he didn't dwell on it and didn't let it eat at him. He knew that he'd get there, just like I knew I'd get to Notre Dame. He just had to keep working and putting up the numbers.

Another thing these players have in common is that when their chance came, they were ready. They had set goals along the way and had gotten better every day. They had learned their craft and used their time in baseball's mail room well.

Here's another rule:

Patience is still a virtue.

One of the biggest problems with our society is the constant reinforcement of the notion that we have to have everything NOW! Too many kids would rather sell drugs or steal than pay attention in school because they think they have to have everything now. Television is an unrelenting bombardment of advertising, all of it dedicated to making us want to have everything this minute. And some of our biggest crooks aren't the drug dealers but the inside traders who care about nothing but making as many millions as possible.

So we get out of school and we get a job and immediately we want it all. People who just have to make a mortgage payment want to pay for the whole house. A good used car won't do, as it did for our parents. We want the turbocharged sports coupe. *And* the skiing holiday in Aspen. *And* the cellular phone. *And* the hot tub. *And* the Rolex watch.

In the 1980s, a lot of kids went to college and took up majors that they thought would pay them the most money instead of give them the most enjoyment and satisfaction. Today, you meet those same kids, grown up now, and they can't stand their jobs, because they never wanted them in the first place. They just wanted the instant gratification.

Maybe they had a dream once, but when it didn't come true in a year or two, they gave up. They didn't have time to wait for what they really wanted, so they took whatever was available.

Maybe it looked good at the time, but there's a horrible price to pay. It's when you wake up and you're forty years old and you realize you hate what you're doing. It's when you're thirty-five and get hit in the face with the realization that you never wanted to be a bond salesman. You really wanted to be a marine biologist, and now what do you do?

What you do is step back and evaluate yourself and your life. See where you are and where you really want to be. And realize it's never too late to do it.

But this time, do it right. Get that big dream up there and then set your daily, weekly, monthly, and yearly goals. Go to work with a smile on your face. Be ready when the time comes.

And work, work, and work some more.

That's another rule:

You can never work too hard.

By that, I don't mean you have to be a drudge; that there is no time for fun. Nobody worked harder than I did on the Notre Dame football team, but even I didn't go full-bore every minute of every day. I'd have been dead if I had. You have to program down time, take mini-vacations. That might mean shutting down for an afternoon or a day and instead of working, clearing your mind. It's like catching your mental breath. On the practice field, it might mean relaxing for only a few minutes, but that can be enough.

But when it comes time to pay the price, you have to be there. You have to know how to dig down deep and come up with as much as you need. I guess you could say that the reason I was successful enough in football to make the team was because I could dig deeper than anyone else.

Coaches and fans and players call that heart. People ask me, "Rudy, how do I get that kind of heart?" Well, how does anybody get it? How did I get it?

I just wanted it. That's all. And it's all that you have to do. You've got to want it.

I don't know what it is you want, but I know it's something better than what you have. But you can't think you want something and hope that it happens, because it never will. You have to know deep in your gut that you want it and commit to the long haul. You've got to put time out of your mind. And when you make that kind of commitment, then good things happen.

The measure of your commitment is work. You can call that persistence if you want, because that's what it comes down to. If you're persistent, you'll do everything that's necessary. Someone looking at you from the outside might think, "Wow, look at that guy work!" But from the inside, it won't seem like work at all, because this is your dream you're dealing with. You're just going after it.

For me, it just kept kicking in like higher gears on a car. From desire came commitment came perseverance came persistence came patience.

Patience was the hardest. I wasn't any different from anyone else. I wanted it right away, too. That's why even though Brother John told me I had to put in two years at

Holy Cross, I applied to Notre Dame after one year. I didn't have patience. It set me up for a major disappointment, but when I put in that second year and got into school, I began to understand what Brother John was talking about. I began to get patience.

That's a big factor in sports. Coaches talk about patience all the time. If you want to win the Super Bowl, you don't go out and throw the ball sixty yards every play hoping you'll score a touchdown on every play. It doesn't work that way. You take what the other team will give you, and if that means nibbling your way downfield four or five yards at a time, that's what you do. And when they finally start crowding the line to stop you, that's when you go deep. And now it will work, because you've been patient.

Baseball players are very patient. The hitter who goes to the plate and tries to hit every pitch out of the park won't last a week. Even the great home-run hitters wait for the pitch they want; the one they can blast over the wall.

In hockey, you'll hear coaches tell their players to be patient on a power play. You look at a hockey game and you wonder, "How can anyone be patient at the speed they're going?" But what the coach means is waiting that extra split second before firing. It's the split second when the goalie commits and leaves the net open.

Life works the same way. You don't go out and meet the man or woman of your dreams and propose marriage in the first ten minutes of your first date. You have to be patient; let things develop.

Salesmen have to have a great deal of patience. In a business like real estate, it takes years of patient and persistent work to build up the customer trust and familiarity that leads to success. You can't just grab people who walk in off the street and say, "Buy this house now, or else!" You'll chase them away.

No, you have to spend a lot of time putting your name in front of them. You send them mailers. You wish them Merry Christmas. If they're looking for the perfect house, you don't bother them with every new listing that comes in, but you wait until you have one that matches their dreams. Then you call them. And the more customers you do that with, the more word will get around; the more credibility you'll have.

I got a movie made. Now people call me up with movie ideas and send me scripts. If I had told anyone five years ago that things like that would be happening to me, they'd have laughed in my face.

But that was when all I had was a dream. Then, a lot of people thought I was a pest, because I didn't just disappear when they turned me down the first time. And I guess if that's your definition of a pest, then that's what I was.

But when people told me to go away initially, they were really saying they didn't want to deal with a new idea. They were hoping I would go away, because that would make their lives a whole lot easier. They wouldn't have to deal with something that was unfamiliar to them.

Like a good real estate agent, I didn't just keep calling. I went home and worked harder. When I came up with a new idea or a new angle, I called back.

It's not easy to call back. Especially when you know people think you're a pest. We all want to be liked. I still struggle with that. I deal with it by continually reminding myself what my purpose is. And if reaching my dream means calling someone back who doesn't want to hear from me, I'll call him back. But only when I have a new approach or new information.

You have to be sensitive to other people. You have to realize when you're being a pain in the neck. You can tell that from their tone of voice; their body language.

If you know who you are and what you're pursuing, you'll realize you don't care if they think you're a pain. You came to that office or made that phone call for a purpose. Once you have that, you override your discomfort. It stops being an obstacle.

But again, you can't just call and call and call. You have to have patience. You have to give things time to happen.

After the first time I met Angelo Pizzo and he told me he didn't like Notre Dame and he wasn't going to do another Indiana sports movie, it took two more years before he finished the script. During that time, every couple of months or so—whenever I got fresh information—I'd feed it to him. At first, Angelo thought I was a pain. He doesn't anymore.

But I could have given up after the first time I talked to him. I could have said, "Well, that dream's gone."

I didn't, because I had no time limit. All I had was a willingness to work and work and work until somehow I got it done. And today, people who think I know all about making movies send me scripts.

I didn't get any smarter. But it isn't about being smart. Who knows how smart Thomas Edison was? All we really know is that Edison was willing to work harder than anyone, and he didn't quit when he hit a dead end. He went through thousands of substances before he discovered the filament that made his light bulb work. Somebody else would have given up. But Edison wanted to make a light bulb. He knew it would work. All he had to do was find that magic filament, and he was willing to keep going until he did.

It was Edison who said that genius is 10 percent inspiration and 90 percent perspiration. What he didn't say is that the inspiration comes up front. The perspiration follows. And Edison could outwork anyone. He used to keep going for two or three days at a time and then sleep in his laboratory.

The way I see it, Edison didn't think of what he was doing as work. He saw it as chasing dreams. And when you're doing that with everything you have inside you, time disappears. All that exists is the quest.

RUDY'S RULE # 9

Never Quit

I keep talking about perseverance and persistence and patience. I talk about sticking with it and not quitting. And maybe you're sitting there saying, "Oh, sure. That's easy for him to say. He's just one of those guys who doesn't know when he's beat. He's not bright enough to quit."

That's just not true. For most of my life, I was a quitter. I quit almost everything I ever tried.

I even quit the Notre Dame football team.

I quit less than two days before the final game of my senior year. Everything I had worked for and dreamed about for nearly ten years I threw away in a selfish fit of negative anger and disappointment.

Thanks to some wonderful friends, it didn't take long to realize what a jackass I was. But the fact remains I quit, just as I had always quit before.

Although I quit the Thursday before our last game, the seeds were sown a year earlier. That was when Ara Parseghian, one of the greatest coaches in Notre Dame history, retired and was replaced by Dan Devine.

Parseghian had given me the chance to make the team.

And because of the effort I put in on the practice squad my first year, he pretty much promised me that the next year— my last year—he would let me dress for a game.

But at the end of that season, Ara realized that if he kept coaching at Notre Dame, it was going to kill him. That's the kind of pressure that goes with the job. When he left and Coach Devine took over, I was back at square one. Whatever Ara had told me didn't apply anymore.

To Ara, I was the undersized but eager kid who walked into his office two years before he would even be eligible for the team and announced he was going to play for Notre Dame. To Coach Devine, I was just another guy on the practice squad. There were forty others just like me.

This is no criticism of Devine. He had to win football games. And the harsh fact of life in college football is that there are about a hundred kids on the team, but the rules allow only sixty to dress for each game. I knew this, but I figured that somehow, I'd work harder than everyone and get to dress for just one game.

Game after game went by until there was only one left, against Georgia Tech. No one told me I would dress, but this was my dream, and I knew it had to come true then or it never would. I had invited my father up to see me run out onto the field. I told everyone this was the week. It made sense. The last game of the season was when the seniors on the practice squad finally got their chance.

The names of the players who would dress for each game were posted in the locker room after Thursday's practice. Each week I had gone to that list looking for my name. Each week it hadn't been there. But this was the last week. This time, Rudy Ruettiger had to be on that list.

I ran in after practice and went straight to the dress list. I scanned it once. No Rudy. I read it again, more slowly. Still no Rudy. Again and again I kept reading it, hoping that somehow I had missed my name; that somehow, if I stared at it long enough, my name would magically appear.

It wouldn't, of course, and I knew it. But I couldn't stop staring at it. And as the searing reality burned into my soul, the tears began running down my face.

My teammates saw me there, and as they walked past to see their own names, they patted me on the shoulder. "Rudy, it's okay, man." And "You'll be all right, Rudy."

Bull. It wasn't okay, and I wasn't going to be all right. I had invested my life into pulling on that uniform and running out of that tunnel onto the perfect green grass of Notre Dame Stadium. I had killed myself in practice, forcing myself to keep going through pain and fatigue day after day. I had given everything I had, and these no-good bleeps weren't going to let me have that one simple reward.

For two years I'd been telling everyone back home in Joliet that I was on the Notre Dame football team, and they replied sarcastically, "If you're on the team, how come we don't see you on television?" And "How come your name's not in the program?"

I had become something of a campus hero the year before, when I went out for the Bengal Bouts, Notre Dame's annual St. Patrick's Day amateur boxing tournament. I had fought the year before, too, but when they found out I wasn't a student, I'd been disqualified. But then I had won. A lot of prestige went along with that, especially on the football team. Then, in my senior year, the local newspaper had even done a story on Rudy Ruettiger, the overaged, undersized kid who had a dream. And now it wasn't going to come true.

I cursed everybody in that place. Screw 'em, I screamed. I've given them everything and this is what I get? I quit. I'm not ever coming back to this bleeping place.

And I wasn't, either. That was it. I was history.

My friends saved me. Like in the movie, my friends came to me Friday and asked me what was wrong. Friday was when we had a walk-through practice in dress uniforms, and the last Friday of the season was when the team picture was taken. I had quit, so I wasn't going to dress, not even for the picture.

One of the guys was a janitor. From everyone, the message was the same.

"There's greater tragedies in life than not getting on the dress list," my friend, the janitor, told me. In the movie, Charles Dutton plays the janitor.

"But I wanted to run through that tunnel to prove to my dad, prove to everyone, that I was on the team."

"Prove what?" he said. "You got nothing to prove to anyone. You stood out there for two years with the best team there is. You've proved you belong. That's all that counts. Forget the uniform."

Another friend, also a janitor, told me, "Rudy, you can't quit."

"I can do anything I want," I said, pouting and angry like a little kid.

"This is your dream, man," he said. "Don't let them take it from you. If you don't go back out there, there won't be a day in your life when you won't regret it."

I had been just hanging around. Practice had already started. And what I didn't know is that four of my senior teammates had gone to the assistant coaches and volunteered to forfeit their places on the roster so that I could dress. In the movie, the whole team lays their jerseys on Devine's desk. In real life, it wasn't quite that dramatic, but it was just as impressive, maybe more so. Because the guys who gave up their jerseys were scrubs like me who were never going to get another chance to dress. And they sacrificed not only for me, but for another practice squadder who had been left off the dress list for the last time.

They gave their jerseys to the assistants, and the assistants told Devine what had happened. Devine wasn't being mean. Georgia Tech was a tough opponent, and if he had only sixty guys to dress, he wanted them to be his best players. There's not a lot of room in big-time football for sentiment. But when he saw what the team wanted, Coach Devine said, "Okay, let him dress."

If I had known all that, I would have been in that locker room four hours before practice. But I didn't. And out of my anger and spite, I wasn't going to see it through to the end; wasn't going to give myself that last chance.

But what my friends said made me understand how wrong I was. Yes, my dream was to dress, but that wasn't what it was all about. It was about finishing what I had started. My real dream had been to participate, and I had done that. I couldn't throw that away and be remembered as the kid who put himself ahead of the team.

I hurried down to the locker room and got dressed. Everyone else was out on the field, already circled around Coach Devine as practice was almost over by the time I got out. But when I trotted onto the field and they saw me, everything stopped and they started applauding. Coach Devine announced that he wanted all seniors at the pep rally whether they dressed or not, and then "we decided to dress Rudy for the game," he said. I got in the team picture.

The next day I led the team out onto the field, and it was the greatest feeling ever. As the game went on, it happened just like in the movie. We had a slim lead and scored an insurance touchdown late. First my teammates on the sideline and then the whole stadium started chanting, "Ru-dy! Ru-dy! Ru-dy!"

Up in the stands, my father was watching it all when someone next to him said, "Who's this Rudy?" And my Dad said, "That's my son!"

I got in and, on my last chance, I sacked the quarterback. And when the gun sounded to end the game, the crowd roared and my teammates hoisted me on their shoulders and carried me off the field. Just like in the movie.

Wow! How do you top that? How do you even describe it? And even while it was happening, I was thinking about how I had quit less than two days earlier, and if it hadn't been for my friends, this would never have happened.

I had quit, but I hadn't quit after all. It was the first time in my life I had stuck something through to the bitter end, come what may.

What a lesson and what a way to learn it!

Never quit, man. Just never, never quit.

You see, you can think it's over, but it isn't necessarily so. Like Yogi Berra said, it ain't over 'til it's over.

When I was so heartbroken when the dress list went up, I thought that I had done everything I could do. I thought I had given 100 percent and there wasn't anything left. And so I quit.

But I hadn't done everything. There was still that Friday walk-through and the picture. And as long as there's one shred of time, one small something that you haven't yet done, you haven't given 100 percent. If you quit then, you're cheating yourself. My friends were right. I would have regretted that forever, because even if it had turned out that I didn't get to dress, at least I would have seen it to the end.

By seeing it to the end, at least I would have been certain. And I would have been able to sit down years later and not have a single regret because I had given it everything and it didn't happen. But I would have had my dream. I had been on the team. I graduated from Notre Dame.

It turned out even better, but that's what happens when you don't quit.

It's like the 1992 National Football League playoffs when the Buffalo Bills were down 28-3 at the half and 35-3 at the beginning of the third quarter. Everyone in the stadium knew it was over. The sportswriters were sitting in the press box getting an early start on their stories about how the Oilers blew away the Bills. Even the television announcers, who are trained to try to maintain excitement long after a game has been decided, had given up on the Bills.

The only people in the entire country who hadn't given up were the only ones who mattered—the Bills themselves. Final score: Bills 41, Oilers 38. It was the greatest comeback in National Football League history.

Odds are it will be forty or fifty years before another team stages a comeback to beat that one. It's not going to happen every time. But the glory, as I found out, is not so much in getting there as in the journey. And if you sit back when things look darkest and say, "It's not going to happen," you have no chance at all. But as long as you're out there trying, you still have that chance. It may be a million to one, but that's better than no chance at all.

That's all you want—a chance. But what we too often fail to see is that the idea isn't to sit around and wait for a chance. You make your own chances, just like you make your own luck. The chance is always there. The question is, are you going to be ready for it? Or are you going to quit?

If that's the only thing you get from my story, that's enough. Never quit.

That's why President Clinton liked *Rudy* so much. He's a Rudy, too. When I went to the White House, he told me how he had lost his first reelection campaign as governor of Arkansas. He could have quit right there. He'd had his moment in the sun and then he failed. But he used that failure as a learning experience and he went right back to work. He did it because he hadn't reached his dream yet.

The president also told me about how he enjoys going back to his high school reunions. He doesn't go because he wants to show off or anything like that. He goes because he had a classmate who's a world-class dreamer. This guy has failed over and over again. He's been bankrupt a number of times. But every time President Clinton sees him, he's full of enthusiasm. He's always got a new dream going, and this time he's going to make it work. He's someone with every reason to quit, but not only does he keep going, but he loves every minute of it. President Clinton told me that's why he goes to the reunions—because he can't wait to hear what his old friend is up to. This guy keeps trying while others get a job, find a comfort level, and stay there forever, playing it safe, not taking risks, not daring to dream.

The president's friend understands what life is all about. It's a journey, and most of the fun is in getting there. Like most journeys, it doesn't always go the way you planned. So here's another rule to keep in mind:

Never quit, but know when to stop.

This is so important. If you go out and just keep going straight ahead, sooner or later, you're going to get very frustrated. It's like going through a maze. Sometimes you get to dead ends. Or it's like driving down a country road and finding a tree lying across it. You can't drive through the tree. You have to come up with another plan.

When I say never quit, that doesn't mean you never stop. It means you never quit trying. Just because you've hit a dead end and stopped doesn't mean you've quit. But if you hit that dead end in the dark of night, it makes more sense to wait until daylight to find out where you are rather than running around blind bumping into more walls.

Some people confuse stopping with quitting, like they've done all they can in one day or one week and they're too tired to do any more. And that's true. It happens to everyone. The last pitcher to win thirty games in one season was Denny McLain. He won thirty-one games in 1968. But he also lost six games. Every time he lost, he got stopped. But he didn't quit.

When we were putting the movie together, we got to a point where we had actually sold it. But then the man who bought it changed studios and his old studio dumped all his projects. Suddenly there we were with a movie and no way of getting it made.

We were stopped, but we didn't quit. Through all the connections our team had, we found out that Tri-Star Pictures had an opening in their schedule for a film with a budget that matched ours. The conditions were that the film had to be ready to shoot.

Bingo! We showed up with their film. And even then, there

came a time when Tri-Star said, "We're sorry, Rudy. We just can't do it."

That's the end of it, right?

Wrong. It meant we were stopped for a while, but we went out and developed more information. This is where Angelo Pizzo, David Anspaugh, Robert Fried, and Cary Woods—the writer, director, and producers—really saved the project. I could only do so much myself, but I didn't know Hollywood like they did. They were the ones who had to use their experience and muscle to overcome the objections and doubts of the studios. We answered their objections, came up with solutions to their problems, and the project was on again.

Tri-Star had probably thought I was finished. And then I'm calling them again. And they're thinking, "Look at that guy. He keeps coming back."

Sometimes, you have to stop and start over at a new beginning. I've done that many times. I've been broke more times than I care to count, and I've started over every time. I truly believe that they can come today and take everything I own and I'll start over and still make it. They may stop me, but they'll never get me to quit on the big picture; on the dream.

There was a time before I really got going on my movie dream when I had lost another job and was so broke I also lost my apartment. I heard that a good business to go into was the cleaning business. I called my brother Mick, who had just graduated from college, and my brother John, and asked them if they wanted to come out to Baltimore, where I was living, and help me start the business.

They came out thinking they was going to find me living in a big house and driving a swell car. Instead, I was living in the attic of a big house and driving a car that we had to push to get started every morning. I didn't have a nickel for rent, but I had an idea that it was going to work. We didn't have a shower, so I joined the YMCA and showered there. And when it got too cold to sleep in the attic, I got an account with my doctor and I made his office the last one I cleaned. Then I slept on his couch for a couple hours.

We worked our tails off on that cleaning business and eventually we made it work. One of our clients—a realtor—had an old farmhouse that he let us live in. We still didn't have any water, because the pipes all burst. But we had a roof. Finally, we had enough success to move into a first-rate apartment.

We kept it up for a couple of years, but ended up selling the business. John and Mick realized they didn't want to do that all their lives. They both really wanted to be high school coaches. So that's what they became. And I was getting this idea about making a movie about my life.

Some people can look at that story and say that I quit. But all I did was sell a business. I stopped to regroup and think about what I really wanted to be doing, and it wasn't staying up all night cleaning toilets. There were other jobs out there I could do to help me get there.

When you stop and take stock, you're being flexible. You're not stuck on one route and one set of rules. You planned that route and made those rules for a reason, but if they no longer fit your situation, you have to be ready to change them. What remains unchanged is your final destination; your dream.

As long as you stay focused on that final destination and don't quit, you remain in control. You stop looking at rejection as defeat. Instead, it's just another roadblock you have to go around.

So you stop counting rejections. You're a salesman and the customer says no. So what? If you're rejected, maybe it's just not the right time. Maybe you don't have the knowledge you need yet. Maybe you need to change your game plan. But you don't quit, because if you're never turned down it means you're not trying. And if you don't try, you can't make that sale. If someone tells you he or she has gone through life without ever being rejected, don't look at it as a sign of triumph. It only means that person hasn't been trying.

Even when you're running into dead ends, you're making progress. You're learning what not to do, for one thing. For another, you're making contacts, meeting people, getting your name out there.

That's why the six years I spent trying to get *Rudy* made weren't wasted. Hollywood is a very tight society. Everybody knows everyone else, and there are few secrets. After a while, I had talked to so many people that everyone knew about the project. That's key in Hollywood. It doesn't matter whether they said I was good or bad. At least they knew who I was. When it finally came together, it was easier because of that.

I didn't invent any of this. I had learned about not quitting on the football field and in the classroom. But what got me going on the movie—I mean really going and fully committed to it—was the movie *Rocky*. I was watching it on tape with my stepdaughter, Cheryl. I had all my Notre Dame stuff on the walls, and I thought that my story was like Rocky's—Rocky with cleats.

I had been dealing with a lot of frustration and confusion in my life. But watching *Rocky* gave me that kick in the backside, that jolt of determination. I was ready to slurp raw eggs, go out and run up the museum steps, do whatever it took.

I was so enthused that I traced Stallone's roots in Maryland. He had lived on a farm and his mother was a hairdresser. I found the farm, just to see where he came from.

When he made *Rocky,* he didn't have any money either. All he had was that dream. As a moviemaker, he really was Rocky Balboa, an obscure nobody looking for his shot at the big time.

I never tried to contact Stallone. I didn't know how, although if I had to, I would have found a way. Years later I went to a trade show the movie industry has every year in Las Vegas—Show West. It's a chance for exhibitors and filmmakers to get together. The studios put together trailers for their season of films and sell them to the theaters. It's a really big show and all the stars and the directors and producers show up to help sell their movies.

And that's how I finally met Sylvester Stallone, who also

had a movie, *Cliffhanger*, out with Tri-Star. When I met him in Hollywood before we all flew to Vegas, I told him about how I had researched his life and how he had inspired me. The next thing I know, I'm riding in a limo with him to the airport and he's talking movie-making with me.

We had a private plane waiting at the airport, and when I got on, I didn't try to sit with Stallone. I figured I had had my time and it wouldn't be right to force myself on him. But when he got on, he came back and sat with me. He could have sat anywhere, but he sat with me because he wanted to learn more about my story. That's how he got so far, by talking to as many people as he could and never thinking he knew it all.

Besides, he identified with me, because if I was a Rocky, he was a Rudy. We both came from the same place. And the fact that I had a grass-cutting job to go back to in South Bend didn't bother him at all.

That's what happens when you don't quit. When it finally comes together, all these doors that were closed to you are flung open. Your universe expands, and with it comes a whole new world of opportunity.

Even if *Rudy* had not become a feature film, I still would have pursued a career as a public speaker. I had thought about that since I was a kid. I would have made it, too, at some level. But getting the movie done made it happen so much faster. You see it all the time with athletes and movie stars and businessmen.

Take a guy like Bob Hoskins. Here was a serious stage actor in England who was virtually unknown by the world at large. He was middle-aged already when Disney Studios started looking for an outstanding actor to star alongside a cartoon rabbit in *Who Killed Roger Rabbit?*

They wanted somebody who didn't have a big name, because they didn't want the human actors to be bigger than the cartoon characters. Hoskins was the man.

He played the role perfectly, and suddenly, the entire world knew what a fine actor he was. Doors opened all over

Hollywood. Now, Bob Hoskins has all the big-budget work he wants. And he can still do his serious stage roles.

But even if that role hadn't come along, Bob Hoskins was doing what he wanted to do. He was acting, and he wasn't going to quit just because he wasn't getting fabulously wealthy.

Actors are like writers and musicians. They do it because they love it. They may dream about hitting the big time, but they don't quit just because they've worked at it a number of years and are still doing summer stock, or playing in high school gyms, or writing good books that just don't take off.

That's the only way you can go about the dream business. You do it and keep doing it because it's what you are. Maybe you go ten years doing good work and you don't hit the bestsellers list or get a platinum record or land that starring role. But if you quit, it's over. You'll never get there. All you can do is keep putting yourself out there, doing the best you can each and every day.

Here's another thing to remember along the way:

It's all right to grieve over your failures.

I call it grief rather than depression. Because that's the way I look at setbacks. You try something and it doesn't work. You have to take time, whether it's a few minutes, hours, or days, to grieve that loss. You have to let yourself cry. It's like holding a small, private wake for an effort that died. It's a personal loss, and you feel down. So you grieve and then you go on.

A man who knows what that's all about is Dan Reeves. He's a football coach, now with the New York Giants after a lengthy stint with the Denver Broncos. He's an outstanding coach, too, but he's never had a season that's ended with his ultimate dream fulfilled.

As a player, Reeves played with the Dallas Cowboys in one of the greatest games in the history of the National Football League. That was the so-called "Ice Bowl" in Green Bay against the Packers for the championship of the 1966 NFL season. A halfback, Reeves threw an option pass for the touchdown that put the Cowboys ahead on a bitterly cold day. But on the last play of the game, Bart Starr, the Green Bay quarterback, snuck into the end zone for the touchdown that won the game.

As a coach, it was more of the same. Three times he got the Denver Broncos to the Super Bowl and three times they lost. It wasn't for lack of effort or will. They got beat by better teams who wanted it every bit as badly as the Broncos did.

The Broncos finally let Reeves go, and he left with the stigma of being a loser. He had plenty of money and could have retired, but that wasn't what he wanted. He wanted that championship. When the Giants offered him their head coaching job, he took it.

In one year, Reeves took the Giants from thorough mediocrity to the playoffs. He didn't get to the Super Bowl, but he got more out of his team than anyone had thought was possible.

He wasn't happy when the year ended, because, once again, he didn't have the championship ring that defines his coaching dream. But he didn't quit, either. And he won't quit. The critics can say anything they want. The fact remains that Dan Reeves is a winner.

What Reeves has is faith—faith in himself and faith in a power higher than himself. He was raised with values that he teaches his players. His teams play clean and they play hard. You have to admire someone like that.

Reeves is like President Clinton. Both refuse to give up on themselves. They've surrounded themselves with positive people who share their dreams. That's another thing the president said to me. "If it wasn't for all my friends," he said, "I wouldn't be here. I should have quit when I didn't get reelected governor. But if I had quit, I wouldn't be president.

"Even now, today, they keep throwing obstacles at me. And I have to handle them."

You don't have to be president or win the Super Bowl. You

don't have to make a movie or play for Notre Dame. You don't have to be president of General Motors. But you can be like these men.

You just have to stay with it. Be flexible, have faith, work your tail off, and don't quit. I think about it all the time. Man, what if I had walked out of that locker room and not come back? The thrill I had when I was carried off that field never would have happened. I'd have been left with woulda, coulda, shoulda.

I think about all the times I should have quit and I didn't. If I'm proud of one thing, that's it.

I got stopped, I got down, I changed game plans, I hit dead ends, but I didn't quit.

Everything I've done since that last Friday of my football career is because of that.

RUDY'S RULE #10

When You Achieve One Dream, Dream Another

10

When I made my tackle and they carried me off the field, I thought that was it. I mean, what more could there be? I figured God was going to come down right there and take me straight to heaven. For all I knew, I was already there.

As far as that went, I wouldn't have cared if I had nailed the quarterback and gotten killed on the same play. They could have put me in a box right then, said, "See ya later, Rudy," and I wouldn't have objected a bit. It still would have been a heck of a movie, although somebody else would have had to make it.

But God didn't take me to heaven. Instead, I went into the locker room with everyone else, took off my uniform, and that was the end of the season.

The thrill lasted a long time. I was something of a campus celebrity, and I cruised through the rest of the school year.

In June, I got my degree, and then reality smacked me in the face again. And the reality was I didn't have a focus anymore; didn't have a dream. Not only didn't I have a dream,

I didn't have a clue as to what I was going to do.

But I had to do something. I was out the door and in the street, just like that, diploma in hand. The power plant was out. That much I knew. But what now?

Well, I had to get a job. I was a pretty good talker and eager enough, so I went into insurance as a salesman. I did all right at it, because I had that enthusiasm and persistence. I got my nifty car, and did all the things you're supposed to do to take your mind off the fact that you don't have a dream anymore. And because of that, I'd lose interest in whatever job I had and I'd get into something else.

That only lasts so long. I needed to do something extraordinary. I had always had this idea that I could become a public speaker, but I needed a reason for people to listen to me. And puttering along from job to job wasn't going to do it.

The truth was that I had already done something extraordinary. I had given life to a dream, chased it down, and lived it. But I hadn't yet absorbed the lesson from what I had done.

It's obvious looking back. I needed another dream; something to put me out there on the edge again, where the intensity of the ups and downs consumes you and makes you as alive as you can ever be. I'm not the type to go rock climbing or hang gliding or scuba diving to fill that need for risk. My risks and challenges have to be mental and spiritual. And they have to involve other people.

The greatest pleasures are those that are shared with others. That's what football and Notre Dame had given me. I hadn't wanted to be the superstar. I had just wanted to be part of it, to participate in a great legend and tradition. If I could sit back when it was over and honestly say that I had helped to make my teammates better, that I had contributed to the success of the team, that was enough. The rest was gravy. It was very rich gravy, but it was still gravy.

Selling insurance didn't do it for me. There's nothing wrong with it. It just didn't jibe with what I wanted. It didn't fill that huge emptiness that the realization of my Notre Dame dream had left.

I had come face to face with the old cliché: Be careful what you wish for. You just may get it.

And once you get it, what do you do next?

Sitting with my stepdaughter and watching *Rocky* made me understand that what I wanted to do next was go after another dream. It had to be a big dream, and making a movie was it.

It took six years, but now I finally had the secret. And this time, when I achieved my goal, I wasn't going to sit back and fall back into that void. Long before *Rudy* hit the big screen, I knew what would be next.

I was going to become a public speaker. This was another extraordinary dream. At least for me, it is. I speak with a bit of a lisp and instead of being tall and built like a model for Italian suits, I'm short and square. I know my grammar isn't always perfect, and sometimes, because of my dyslexia, I don't pronounce a word the way they have it in the dictionary.

But that's what makes it fun, because there are people who think they know me who don't think I can do it. It's my old "I'll show them" reflex at work.

But that wasn't all. I was also going to write a book. And it doesn't end there. I'm bursting with dreams now. I want to write a novel and make another movie, this time one that's not about me. I want to cut the grass in Notre Dame Stadium.

I always knew I had to do something, but now I realize that as long as I have to work, I may as well do things I want to do. And it doesn't matter what others think about my ideas. I'm the one who's keeping score, not them.

I don't know if I'll be a motivational speaker forever. If someone were to ask me what my niche is in life, I'd have to say I don't really know.

But I know that I still have a way to go in my new dream job. And that's great. It's a big challenge to get up in front of a roomful of people and help them to believe in themselves.

I've had people who've asked to coach me. "Rudy, I'll make you a great speaker," they say.

But no one can teach you that. You can be coached, but then all you're going to be is what the coach makes you. He can help you with how to construct a speech and the mannerisms and the way you dress. But to me the key to public speaking is getting way down deep inside and letting it come out. Nobody can give you those words. They have to come from you.

If I have a strength as a speaker, that's it. I speak from my heart. A lot of people speak from a base of research. I speak from experience. I've been where you are and where you've been. I know where you want to go. I know what it's like to reach for improbable goals. I know what it's like to suffer confusion and despair. And I know it's worth it to see it through.

Like I said at the start, there's millions of Rudys out there. Most of you reading this book probably have more natural ability than I do. So you can do it. Your dreams are waiting for you to find them.

You just have to know how to go about it.

It starts with sitting yourself down for a personal heart-to-heart talk. Who are you? Not the person other people want you to be or the person they think you are. But who are you really? Remember, it's your life and it's up to you to take charge of it.

If you've been dumped on, knocked around, or laughed at, don't be afraid of the anger you feel. Embrace it as a friend instead of fearing it as an enemy. Don't let your anger drive you down to the corner tavern and turn you bitter. If half the office gets together at lunch to moan and whine about how miserably they're treated, stop hanging out with them. Hang out with the people who want to succeed and who want you to succeed. Show those people who laughed at you the great things that are inside.

Armed with that motivation and the knowledge of who you really are, let yourself dream. It doesn't matter what you dream. It can be little or big, but make it as large as you dare, and then maybe a little larger. Sort out fantasy from dreams that are possibilities. Make your dream conform to who you are.

Once you've identified your dream, formulate a plan. At the outset, it doesn't have to be complicated. The simplest plan is to just go do it. As you move forward and learn more about your dream, your plan can become more detailed and focused. But don't let confusion and complication stop you before you start.

Don't be afraid to fail. If you don't fail, you're not dreaming big enough. Remember, you can lose a lot of battles and still win the war. The only thing you have to do when you fail is learn from the experience. It's a much greater teacher than success.

Get the dollar signs out of your eyes. If your dream is to get rich, you may do it, but you won't really enjoy it. And usually, you'll fail. Because you've set yourself up for failure. Remember, the sacrifice that goes into fulfilling a dream makes it that much better when it comes. Don't worry about the money. It will come.

There are no excuses. You can't miss practice because you have a hangnail. You can't miss that meeting because you stayed out too late and overslept. When you're chasing dreams, you can't say the dog ate your homework. Remember that knowledge is power.

There is no time limit on dreams. But there is such a thing as timing. When opportunity strikes, it can come out of the blue. When it does, you had better be ready for it. And to get ready, there is no substitute for hard work. Don't run around saying you're giving 110 percent. Give 100 percent. That's all you have. It's all you need.

Don't ever, ever quit. That's the key that holds it all together. If you quit, you go right back with the whiners and complainers; with the people who live their lives in bitterness because of what they woulda, coulda, and shoulda done.

Recognize that stopping now, regrouping to try a new approach isn't quitting. And as long as there is one shred of anything that you can still do—one phone call, one trip to the library, one letter—you have to do it. If you quit, you'll regret it forever.

Finally, be ready to reach your goal, and when you do, have another one waiting to take its place. Getting what you want is only a problem if you have nowhere to go next. Dreaming is a lifetime occupation.

Before I go, I want to share with you a letter that my family gave me at the premier of *Rudy*, September 6, 1993. They had it done up by a calligrapher, and I have it framed in my bedroom.

An Open Letter to Our Brother:

Dear Danny,

Relentless in your pursuit to achieve your
dream people considered impossible and
foolhardy, you persevered.

Undying in your belief that what you thought was
the rejuvenation of your spirit for life and
your peace of mind, you ventured.

Determined in your mind to surpass
the ridicule and mockery that erupts in your path
on and off the field, you overcame.

Yearning in your faith to bring to a nation
the story of one inspired, willing to do what
he believed in his heart, you succeeded.

You have awed your family and sent hope
rippling into the youth of America. Your story
is one of pride, hope, and a willingness to
work for what one truly believes in his heart
and soul.

We love you.

Love,
Mom, Dad, Jeanann, Mary, Carol, Rose, Betsy,
Timmy, Francis, Mickey, Johnny, Rita, Norma,
Bernie, and Mark.

A

LAKE COUNTY PUBLIC LIBRARY
INDIANA